FOLLOW ME

FOLLOW ME

A 52/7 Journey of Discipleship

Phil McKinney II, Ph.D.
with the Fairfax Church of Christ Discipleship Team

Follow Me: A 52/7 Journey of Discipleship
Copyright © 2017 by Phil McKinney II, Ph.D., and the Fairfax Church of Christ

All rights reserved. Printed in the United States of America. No part of this book may be used or reproduced in any manner whatsoever without written permission except in the case of brief quotations embodied in critical articles or reviews.

Unless otherwise identified, Scripture references were taken from the English Standard Version of the Bible.

For information contact:
Fairfax Church of Christ
3901 Rugby Rd.
Fairfax, VA 22033
703-631-2100
http://www.fxcc.org

Book and Cover design by Ashley Young
ISBN: 978-1542956802

First Edition: January 2017

10 9 8 7 6 5 4 3 2 1

Contents

Preface   vii

Chapter 1: Introduction   1
Chapter 2: Two Truths—D²   17
Chapter 3: Huh? What Does That Mean?   25
Chapter 4: Holy and Wholly Living "Do You Love Me?"   33
Chapter 5: What Does a Disciple Look Like?   49
Chapter 6: Developing a Plan for Spiritual Growth   55
Chapter 7: The Plan for Discipleship   89

Appendix A: Resources for Discipleship and Spiritual Formation   105
Appendix B: Not on Bread Alone Menu   123
Appendix C: Six-Year Scope and Sequence   137
Appendix D: Covered in Dust: A Journey in Discipleship   145
Appendix E: What Our Family Believes   147
Appendix F: FXCC Vision, Mission, Values   151

Preface

The book you hold in your hands is the product of a long journey that began in the fall of 2008. As I began my ministry at Fairfax Church of Christ (FXCC), I was asked to add on to my role the oversight of spiritual formation and discipleship. I was blessed to begin this journey with a team of people who desperately wanted to see our church family grow more in their faith and in their relationship with God. There had already been many discussions on this topic before my arrival, but when we all came together, God began to share with our team a vision for spiritual formation and discipleship at Fairfax. We didn't know how it would look specifically, but we knew we had to be faithful to it.

And so we spent six months praying, fasting, studying, and seeking the guidance of the Holy Spirit. After that time of discovery, God laid out for us a plan for spiritual formation and discipleship. We began to share that plan with our leadership, our ministry leads, and finally the entire congregation in the spring and fall of 2009. There was a great deal of excitement as we shared with everyone how we wanted to be intentional with our spiritual growth. We began to implement several aspects of the plan, yet we knew that the aspects were only the beginning steps and that God would continue to shape the plan and show us what He wanted for His people at Fairfax.

Eight years later, we have now revised and edited the plan several times, and you hold the end result of that journey. We again recognize that God will continue to adapt this plan as He deems fit, but we are confident that this is our path ahead for discipleship at Fairfax Church of Christ. So the book is intended to help all of our family members define and understand what our plan for discipleship is at FXCC. Our goal is to assist each of our family members to become *devoted followers of Jesus Christ who passionately lead others to Him.*

It is our hope that this book will help our members answer the questions of *why* (Introduction and Chapter 1), *what* (Chapters 2–4), and *how* (Chapter 5–6). The Appendixes offer additional information to help members move toward becoming disciples who make disciples. We are excited to offer this book to all of our family members with the hope that it will help each one of them toward a deeper relationship with Christ in which His Holy Spirit forms, conforms, and transforms them into the image of our Lord and Savior, Jesus Christ.

As with any work such as this, there are many people who made it all possible. I would like to first thank God for revealing all of this to us. For me, this journey began at a retreat center where I spent the day in prayer and fasting. There, God began to open up the Scriptures to me in a way that I had never seen before. He continues to do that today, and so I cannot help but thank Him and give Him all the glory and honor for this work. I must also recognize our Discipleship Team at Fairfax Church of Christ (both past and present). When we began this journey it was with a team made up of Bruce Black, Lisa Bosley, Andrea Morris, Dave Palmer, Dwayne Phillips, Darla Robinson, Ellyn Sergio, Dakota Wood, and Sammie and Jill Young. Without these individuals, this plan could not have come about.

As the years have gone on several other individuals have served on our Discipleship Team and have contributed to this work, including Todd Batt, Ray Bingham, Dennis Cesone, Erin Gulick, Deb Holder, Sam Jeffrey, P.J. McGuire, Mike Miller, Logan Morris, Chad Mynatt, Alecia Nault, Benn and Laura Oltmann, Andy Pierce, Rebecca Poole, Paul Reiman, Ken Smith, Rita Strydom, Kyle Symanowitz, Tyler Travis, Carie Whittaker, and Lori Windham. Thank you all so much for your words of wisdom and guidance through this journey together.

I would be remiss if I did not also thank my family and, in particular, my wife, Angie. Through the years, Angie has been patient with me as I was away for conferences, school, meetings, and so much more all for the sake of developing this plan and fostering discipleship at FXCC. Both she and my daughters (Kaylee, Taylor, and Rylie) have sacrificed time with me so that this could come to fruition. Thank you all so much. Words could never express my love and appreciation to these beautiful ladies in my life. I thank my God every time I remember you!

May this work bring glory to God and expand His kingdom here on this earth and on through eternity. Now, let's go!

Phil McKinney II
Discipleship Minister
January 24, 2017

Chapter 1

Introduction

FOLLOW ME! Two words that changed the course of 12 unlikely individuals in the first century. Two words that should also change the course of our lives today. But do they? Do we follow Him in the way that the early disciples chose to follow Him? Do we drop everything (without reservation) to follow Him as our Lord and Savior? Or do we follow Him in name alone? Are we satisfied with wearing the name "Christian" without being transformed by the Holy Spirit into His image? Are we satisfied with being "Christians" who receive the salvation that Jesus gives without becoming the people who Jesus calls us to be?

For too long, churches have based their success on numbers. Success has been measured by how many members the church had, how nice and big their building was, how many people they baptized in a year, or even how big their budget was.[1] However, the true measure of success in any church is not whether there are sufficient numbers, big buildings, many conversions, or large contributions. Measured success in the Lord's church is evidenced by His people being formed, conformed, and transformed into His image.

While this sort of evidence may be difficult to quantify, it is demonstrated in the spiritual fruit that disciples bear in their homes, churches,

---

1. Or what some have termed the "Four B's": Butts, Buildings, Baptisms, and Budgets. See Mike McDaniel's "The Resurgent Church," pg. 99.

and communities at large. The real question that must be answered is thus: "What are we moving people toward?"[2] Are we simply interested in gaining in membership and satisfied with developing people into converts rather than disciples? Or, are we helping every person walk down the path of becoming a true disciple of Christ?

A "convert" is a person who has been persuaded to change his or her religious faith or other beliefs. However, one can easily be a convert without being a disciple who follows Christ with total abandonment. The church has for too long focused on making converts rather than making disciples. As Dallas Willard notes,

> …the making of converts, or church members, has become the mandatory goal of Christian ministers—if even that—while the making of disciples is pushed to the very margins of Christian existence. Many Christian groups simply have no idea what discipleship is and have relegated it to para-church organizations.[3]

He goes on to say that the elephant in the church today is "non-discipleship." Willard says, "The fundamental negative reality among Christian believers now is their failure to be constantly learning how to live their lives in The Kingdom Among Us. And it is an *accepted* reality."[4] We have enabled a division among professing Christians: those who are truly and wholly devoted to Christ and those who maintain a consumer, client-based relationship with Christ and His church.

I once had a professor and mentor say this to me, "What we win them with is what we win them to."[5] That phrase has stuck with me all my years of ministry. For the first ten plus years of ministry, I chose to win people to a consumeristic mind-set of Christ and His church. I was more concerned about acceptance and being liked than with truly helping people become the disciples that Jesus called them to be. I won them to a "Fast Food" Christianity and led them to become members of "The Club of Christ." Let me explain.

---

2. To make the question more personal, ask yourself, "What am I moving toward? Christlikenss or Self-likeness?"

3. Dallas Willard, *The Divine Conspiracy*, eBook edition (New York: HarperCollins, 2009,), 300–301.

4. Ibid., 301.

5. Thank you Dr. Dan Stockstill, professor at Harding University.

Fast Food Christianity

In our consumeristic "me-centered" culture, we are often led to live our lives with a "fast food" mentality. We all know what fast food restaurants offer us—a quick source of less-than quality food right when we want it. But why do we choose fast food? Here are some reasons:

- **Replaces our responsibility**. Fast food replaces our responsibility to prepare and cook our meal. Instead, when we don't feel like cooking, we jump in the car and head to the nearest fast food restaurant. We don't have to work; someone else can do it for us.
- **Cheap**. Fast food is not going to cost us a lot unless we want extra and are willing to pay for it. Yet, even with adding on the extras, fast food is typically not costly.
- **Choices**. With fast food, we can choose from several different options to suit our immediate needs and desires. The choice is ours, from choosing the restaurant to choosing the menu items.
- **Service with no strings attached**. With fast food, not only do we get what we want, we are also served by others with little to no contact. We are not required to form any lasting relationships. We order our food, are served, and move on. If we don't like the service, we complain to the manager. If we don't like the food, we take it back and ask that it be replaced according to our liking. We are not required to offer gratuity.
- **Quick**. Fast food typically lives up to its name. We want it now; we get it now. We make our request and expect it promptly.
- **Drive-through service**. With fast food, if we don't want to go in and sit down, we have the option of simply staying in our car, ordering through a microphone, making our payment, picking up our food, and driving off.

But, what does this have to do with our approach to being a Christian? Consider how our approach to Christ is like our approach to fast food: No investment. No attachments. Just fast delivery with superficial interaction as we want it. Is this our approach to Christ? What might a "Fast Food" approach to Christianity look like?

- **Replaces our responsibility**. Fast Food Christianity replaces our responsibility to grow in our relationship with Christ and live our life for Him. Instead, when we don't feel like doing it ourselves, we jump in the car and head to the nearest church and expect someone else to feed us spiritually. We don't have to work; someone else can do it for us who's paid to do it.

- **Cheap**. Fast Food Christianity is not going to cost us a lot unless we want extra and are willing to pay for it. Yet, even with adding on the extras, Fast Food Christianity is typically not costly and will only require us to serve, to reach out, and to give occasionally (if at all). The amount we serve, reach out, and give is up to us and based on how much time and money we are willing to invest *in the moment*.

- **Choices**. With Fast Food Christianity, we can choose from several different options to suit our immediate needs and desires. The choice is ours—from choosing the church to choosing what and how much we will be involved.

- **Service with no strings attached**. With Fast Food Christianity, not only do we get what we want, but we are also served by others with little to no contact. We are not required to form any lasting relationships. We order off the spiritual menu, are served by those paid to serve (and those other few crazy volunteer-types), and move on. If we don't like the service, we complain to the elders and staff members without volunteering to work to make it better. If we don't like the spiritual food, we take it back and ask that it be replaced according to our liking. If our order still doesn't meet our satisfaction, we move on to another choice.

- **Quick**. Fast Food Christianity typically lives up to its name. We want it now; we get it now. We make our request to the elders and staff members about how and what we would like changed and expect it promptly. We want a quick sermon that meets our immediate needs so we can leave quickly. If it isn't quick and it doesn't get to the point that we want to hear, then we stand up and walk out without paying.

- **Drive-through service**. With Fast Food Christianity, if we don't want to be too involved, we have the option of simply coming in for worship (coming late is an option because we must be at work and school on time all week long, so we need a break from being on time), ordering our worship and spiritual food, making our payment (though only if there's money left or the church is spending the money the way we think it should), picking up our worship and spiritual food, and driving off. Maybe Bible class, but that is optional and don't expect anything else.

No investment. No attachments. Is this how Jesus envisioned His disciples? Is a drive-thru relationship all that the Lord requires of us? Or, is there more to this whole "Follow Me" bit? The Bible makes it very clear what the Lord requires. It shows us what being a disciple of Christ might look like:

- **Responsibility**. TRUE Christianity (being a disciple of Christ) requires us to be responsible for our own spiritual growth and to live a life that honors God and reflects Christ. We can't pawn off our responsibility on anyone else because we have been crucified with Christ. Read Hebrews 5:11–6:3 and Galatians 2:20.
- **Costly**. TRUE Christianity (being a disciple of Christ) costs us EVERYTHING! Our money, our possessions, our time—EVERYTHING is HIS. Our salvation cost Jesus everything! Do you think He requires anything less from us? His grace is free but it wasn't cheap. "You were bought at a price." (1 Corinthians 6:20, 7:23) Read Luke 14:25–33.
- **Only ONE CHOICE**. TRUE Christianity (being a disciple of Christ) affords us only ONE CHOICE: **JESUS**. That choice requires that everything else we do be an honor and glory to Him. It requires that we be at our post as Christians 52/7 (see later in the Introduction for more details on this 52/7 concept). There is no option to be uninvolved. Discipleship requires involvement. Read John 14:6, 15, 21, 23–24 and 1 John 2:3–6.
- **Service with strings attached**. TRUE Christianity (being a disciple of Christ) requires us to serve rather than be served. That service expects us to work with and to develop relationships as part of the body of Christ. We, therefore, build eternal relationships with our brothers and sisters, and it is NOT optional. Everyone is required to serve and build up the kingdom of God. It cannot be delegated to paid staff members and church leadership. Complaining without helping to discover and implement a solution is not an option. And, by the way, the chosen solution may not be according to our

own personal liking. Read Mark 10:42–45; Philippians 2:1–18; and 1 John 3:16–19.

- **Slow and at times painful**. TRUE Christianity (being a disciple of Christ) does not happen fast and is a life-long and eternal process. The seeds we plant and the work we do may never produce fruit in our lifetime. As we labor, we will encounter suffering, pain, and change. Our desires may not be in God's plan and, therefore, will not happen. We must surrender our will to conform to His. Read 1 Corinthians 3:1–15; Philippians 1:3–6; Hebrews 11:32–40; and 1 Peter 1:6–12.
- **Commitment**. TRUE Christianity (being a disciple of Christ) requires TOTAL commitment. God will never be satisfied with part of us. Involvement in Christ and His body is expected. Read Luke 9:23–26 and Hebrews 10:24–25.

This Fast Food Christianity mind-set has deeply impacted Christ's church. It has led us to approach the ministry of the church from a worldly view that contradicts God's intent for His people. Instead of helping people join God's family, the church of Christ, we have helped them become members of The Club of Christ. This concept deserves more explanation.

The Club of Christ

We all know what clubs are. They are associations or organizations that are dedicated to a particular interest or activity. Clubs offer individuals a way to join with other individuals for a common purpose. We often join clubs quickly and easily accept their membership requirements no matter the costs or expectations. So, why do we join clubs?

In considering the answer to this question, I searched what a local country club offered its members. The Country Club of Fairfax, Virginia, offers and requires many things.[6] I discovered that the club offers "family." By family, it means that it offers a wide array of activities that provide an opportunity for members to come together and build

---

6. I accessed the follow information from their website (http://www.ccfairfax.org/) as of 2016.

relationships. They also provide a place where "special events" can be held, such as weddings, special occasions, and meetings and seminars. It boasts that the club has experienced personnel who will be there to assist members with all their needs. It states that "no matter your interest, at the Country Club of Fairfax there is truly something for everyone."

As I read on, I discovered that it offers several types of memberships, from full membership with everything the club offers (including stock options) to tailored memberships to meet individual needs. What I found most interesting is that it offers a "social/house only" membership. One can simply come for the fellowship and community. If you think about it, people are willing to pay to have community. Each of the memberships had requirements and fees that accompanied them.

So, what does all that have to do with discipleship and the ministry of the church? Maybe nothing. Or maybe everything. I began to ask myself, "How is the Fairfax Church of Christ any different than the Country Club of Fairfax?" Consider how this view and approach of a worldly country club might infiltrate how we approach the ministry of the church. What if we ran things like a Club of Christ? What would it look like? Perhaps our website would read:

> The Fairfax Club of Christ is a private, member-owned Club that provides exceptional family-oriented spiritual and social services and activities. As a friendly, family-oriented and welcoming membership, the Fairfax Club of Christ is a true reflection of the diversity of those living and working in the Northern Virginia area and provides something for everyone.
>
> *Family*
>
> The Fairfax Club of Christ provides families with exceptional spiritual and social opportunities. Whether it is our vibrant Student Ministry, our exceptional Children's Ministry and preschool, our exciting Young Adults Ministry, or even our pulsating worship services, there is something for every family member to enjoy. In addition, our outstanding Missions and Outreach programs offer even more opportunities for our members to partake in, including optional mission opportunities and service projects, as well as personal training and Bible classes. With an ongoing and active schedule, the Club is the perfect venue to bring families together.

Special Events

We offer worship services, Bible classes, student and children activities, and so much more with a commitment to excellence to exceed your expectations.

Whether you are planning an age-appropriate activity or a small group Bible study, your event will be created especially for you.

Our experienced ministerial staff will work with you to advise and assist you with the planning of your function and selecting your personal spiritual menu. Here at the Club, your spiritual growth will be exactly the way you desire, as each worship, event, and activity is individually planned and tailored with the most personal attention paid to the smallest detail.

The Fairfax Club of Christ can accommodate large families and all arrangements can be discussed by contacting our Catering Director (I mean our Family Life Minister) who will be delighted to discuss your individual needs.

Activities

The Fairfax Club of Christ provides members numerous opportunities to become involved in our active and enthusiastic community. The activities offered by the Club cater to every age and ability, and provide members with the chance to learn, practice or improve upon their spiritual gifts.

The Club also offers activities that meet other interests as well, from various social outings to our women's and men's ministries, options abound outside of traditional church offerings. No matter your interest, at the Club there is truly something for everyone.

Membership Types

- Full membership (full)

o Worship/Bible classes/Small groups/Service/Missions/Ministry Activities (plus stock [full investment in the family at FXCC])

- Half membership

o Worship/Bible classes/Optional Ministry Activities (partial stock [limited investment in the family at FXCC])

- Pew membership

o Worship/Optional Bible classes (no stock [no investment in the family at FXCC])

***Age-Specific Memberships can be added at an additional fee. See below.*

- Age-Specific Membership

o Children's Ministry (Kid's Worship/Bible classes/Kid activities) (No parental involvement necessary) (Children's Stock)

o Student Ministry (Teen Bible classes/Missions/Service/Teen Activities) (No parental involvement necessary) (Teen Stock)

- Other Ministry Membership (Based on personal needs and desires) (Stock options)

****Contact the church office for membership fees and schedules. We are here to serve YOU!*

Again, we must ask, is this what God envisioned for His people? Is this the bride Christ died for? Or is there more? Why will we quickly and easily join and meet the expectations of the Club of Christ, but hesitantly involve ourselves in the church of Christ? When we read from the following passages, we gain a very different perspective of what and how Jesus pictured His bride, the church.

- John 13:34–35 and all of chapter 17
- Romans 12
- 1 Corinthians 12:12–13, 24–27
- Ephesians 4:1–7, 11–16

Those passages teach us that Jesus sought to unify His disciples under the banner of God. He warned them that the world would hate us because of it, but that we should be in the world, not of it. The passages teach us that the church is the body of Christ and collectively that body should use its gifts to honor and glorify Him and the Father. The passages teach that we should stand firm in our faith in times of joy as well as in times of suffering and adversity (as it will be contrary to the world around us) so that we may all grow up and attain the entire fullness of God. We also learn together that (though the world may ridicule us and encourage us to divide) we must love each other in the same way Christ loved us. And by this love, all humankind would know we belong to Christ, and therefore, many will be drawn to that love. Indeed, we are admonished to live this way.

We are called to be more than Fast Food Christians that belong to The Club of Christ. We must ask ourselves these questions:

- Am I a Fast Food Christian or a TRUE disciple of Christ?
- Am I a member of The Club of Christ or a member of the church of Christ?
- What example am I setting for those who worship with us?
- Would first-century disciples give up their lives for Fast Food Christianity or the Club of Christ? Would you?

We are called by Jesus to something greater. We are called by Jesus to follow Him. But what does He mean by "Follow Me"?

FOLLOW ME: 52:7 to 52:7

FOLLOW ME! In Mark 1:17, we hear Jesus speak those words as He calls His first disciples, "Follow me, and I will make you become fishers of men." Do we follow Jesus the way He intended for us to? If not, then why? Perhaps it is because we do not understand what it truly means to follow Jesus.

In the first century, to hear a rabbi say "follow me" was an extreme honor. An individual would have gone through years of study in the Bible as a child and adolescent. After that time, if a rabbi found someone who had an inclination for further study in God's Word, then the rabbi would ask that individual to continue in his studies by following him (the rabbi) in his everyday walk to learn to become a rabbi. To do this meant to leave everything behind, choosing to follow the rabbi in his daily walk. Why? In order that the individual might become like the rabbi to do what the rabbi does or become who the rabbi is.

Those who didn't make the cut would go on to learn their father's trade and to join the family business. Peter, Andrew, James, and John were all fishermen by trade. They had, therefore, never heard the words "follow me" spoken to them from a rabbi. But, when Jesus (a known rabbi) walked by and called to them saying, "Follow me," they dropped everything. Notice that even the father of James and John (Zebedee) did not question what they did or try to stop them (at least from what we know). Perhaps that is because Zebedee knew what an honor his sons had just been given. They were no longer the ones who "didn't make the cut."

Maybe we don't follow Jesus in the same way the early disciples did because we don't realize what an honor we have been given. None of us have "made the cut," but He calls us anyway. We should all be willing to leave everything behind to follow Him. Yet, we too often see people become "converts" and receive salvation without ever truly becoming disciples. Perhaps we have bought into the lie that Satan has taught us; the lie that says all we must do is "get saved" and that is enough. That we can be a Fast Food Christian and belong to The Club of Christ and all is good.

But all isn't good. We are called to something more, something greater. If we buy into Satan's lie, then all we do is cheapen God's grace and love given to us through Jesus, His only Son. This is called *nominal Christianity*: being a Christian in name and reaping the benefits, but living an unchanged life. That is a travesty!

At Fairfax, the leadership is convinced that there is more than being a Fast Food Christian who is a member of The Club of Christ. We are convinced that Jesus has called us to follow Him, to become His disciples, and to make other disciples. The culmination of that belief is

> Nominal Christianity is what Dietrich Bonhoeffer referred to as "cheap grace."[a] Bonhoeffer gives a very clear picture of what he defines as cheap grace, and he says,
>
>> It is grace without a price, without costs. It is said that the essence of grace is that the bill for it is paid in advance for all time. Everything can be had for free, courtesy of that paid bill. The price paid is infinitely great and, therefore, the possibilities of taking advantage of and wasting grace are also infinitely great. What would grace be, if it were not cheap grace? Cheap grace means grace as doctrine, as principle, as system. It means forgiveness of sins as a general truth; it means God's love as merely a Christian idea of God. Those who affirm it have already had their sins forgiven. The church that teaches this doctrine of grace thereby confers such grace upon itself. The world finds in this church a cheap cover-up for its sins, for which it shows no remorse and from which it has even less desire to be set free. Cheap grace is, thus, denial of God's living word, denial of the incarnation of the word of God.[b]
>
> He goes on to say that, "Cheap grace is grace without discipleship, grace without the cross, grace without the living, incarnate Jesus Christ."[c] May that never be!
>
> a. Dietrich Bonhoeffer, *Discipleship*, v. 4, in *Works* (Minneapolis: Fortress Press, 2010), 43.
> b. Ibid.
> c. Ibid., 44.

found within the pages of this book. It is our desire that as you read you will become convinced—no, convicted—that God calls us to something greater. We hope that you will be called to a higher calling given to you by God's grace through His Son, Jesus. That in the end, you would be willing to drop everything for the sake of Christ.

While I was sitting in a conference, the speaker was focusing on the depths of discipleship. As he spoke, he called everyone to being a disciple 24/7 (living for Jesus 24 hours a day, seven days a week). But, as he said those words, I was being convicted inside. Everything inside me screamed, "THAT'S NOT ENOUGH!" I can easily live for Jesus for a day or a week, but how about every day through the next year. Could I commit to being a true disciple of Christ 52/7 (living for Jesus for 52 weeks, 7 days a week)? When this conviction hit me, I wondered if there were 52:7 passages that spoke to that type of commitment. So, I opened my Bible to a couple of books that I knew had 52 chapters, and here is what I found.

The first book I opened to was Psalms. As I thumbed through the pages, I came to Psalm 52:7 and here is what I read:

"See the man who would not make
>   God his refuge,
> but trusted in the abundance of his riches
>   and sought refuge in his own destruction!"

I sat there thinking to myself, "Wow! This is where we all begin in our journey. We all begin with self-reliance and do not seek God as our refuge but ourselves." But I wondered if that was the only message God was teaching me. So I went to the next book, Isaiah. Here's what I read in Isaiah 52:7:

> "How beautiful upon the mountains
>   are the feet of him who brings good news,
> who publishes peace, who brings good news of happiness,
>   who publishes salvation,
>   who says to Zion, "Your God reigns."

I sat there speechless. Now, you can sit there and say that it was all just a matter of chance, but I do not. In that moment of conviction, I believe that God demonstrated to me the journey of discipleship from beginning to end. It is a journey that begins with self and ends with God. For as one starts by only relying on self, in the end (if they seek God with all their heart, soul, mind, and strength), they will fully rely on God as they bring good news to all the world shouting, "Your God reigns!" It is a 52:7 to 52:7 Journey of Discipleship. It is the sort of journey that Theodore Monod wrote a song about many years ago, titled "None of Self and All of Thee."

It is this 52:7 to 52:7 journey that Jesus calls us to as He cries out, "FOLLOW ME!" It is not a journey we go on to see what we get out of it, but it is instead a journey that we go on to see what we can pour into it. It is not a journey we go on to see what God will give us, but a journey we go on to see what we can give God. Why? So we can answer the honor of His call. The call to become His disciple, His child. The call to become the disciple of the Lord of ALL—the God who created all things, sustains all things, and rules all things.

At Fairfax, we are no longer content with drawing people to Fast Food Christianity who become members of our Club of

---

NONE OF SELF AND ALL OF THEE

Oh, the bitter pain and sorrow
  That a time could ever be,
When I proudly said to Jesus,
  "All of self, and none of Thee."
All of self, and none of Thee,
All of self, and none of Thee,
When I proudly said to Jesus,
  "All of self, and none of Thee."

Yet He found me; I beheld Him
  Bleeding on th' accursed tree,
And my wistful heart said faintly,
  "Some of self, and some of Thee."
Some of self, and some of Thee,
Some of self, and some of Thee,
And my wistful heart said faintly,
  "Some of self, and some of Thee."

Day by day His tender mercy,
  Healing, helping, full and free,
Brought me lower while I whispered,
  "Less of self, and more of Thee."
Less of self, and more of Thee,
Less of self, and more or Thee,
Brought me lower while I whispered,
  "Less of self, and more of Thee."

Higher than the highest heaven,
  Deeper than the deepest sea,
Lord, Thy love at last has conquered:
  "None of self, and all of Thee."
None of self, and all of Thee,
None of self, and all of Thee,
Lord, Thy love at last has conquered:
  "None of self, and all of Thee."

> ### "A Disciple's Renewal" Prayer
>
> O my Savior,
> Help me.
> I am slow to learn,
> so prone to forget,
> so weak to climb;
> I am in the foothills when I should be on the heights;
> I am pained by my graceless heart,
> my prayerless days,
> my poverty of love,
> my laziness in the heavenly race,
> my stained conscience,
> my wasted hours,
> my unspent opportunities.
> I am blind while light shines around me:
> take the scales from my eyes,
> grind to dust my evil heart of unbelief.
> Make it my greatest joy to study You,
> meditate on You,
> gaze on You,
> sit like Mary at Your feet,
> lean like John on Your chest,
> appeal like Peter to Your love,
> count like Paul all things waste compared to knowing You, my Lord.
> Give me increase and progress in grace so that there may be
> more decision in my character,
> more vigor in my purposes,
> more elevation in my life,
> more passion in my devotion,
> more constancy in my zeal.
> As I have a position in the world,
> keep me from making the world my position;
> May I never seek in the creature
> what can be found only in the Creator;
> Let my faith never cease to seek You
> until my faith becomes sight.
> Ride forth in me, O King of Kings
> and Lord of Lords,
> that I may live victoriously,
> and in Your victory, finish my race.[a]
>
> a. Bennett, Arthur, ed., *The Valley of Vision: A Collection of Puritan Prayers & Devotions*, Leather Gift 1st ed., 14th printing (Edinburgh: The Banner of Truth Trust, 2015), 334–35. Updated and revised by Phil McKinney II.

Christ. Instead, we are convinced that we must live into God's Story of Redemption and live into His call to be disciples who make disciples for the sake and honor of Jesus Christ. Will you join us in this privilege, in this honor to live as disciples of Christ. That is what this book is all about. We want to not only share with you the importance of discipleship and why it is the mission of Christ, but to also help you understand our plan toward discipleship that we ask you to join us in.

It is a 52/7 journey. We ask that you take this next year and commit to being a disciple of Christ for 52 weeks, 7 days a week. We will provide help and guidance toward this goal in the following pages and in our developed discipleship curriculum, Covered in Dust. We want to provide you as much support as we can to live your part in God's Story

> **Fellowship of the Unashamed**
>
> This letter was found in the office of a young minister in Zimbabwe, Africa following his martyrdom for Christ.
>
> > I'm part of the fellowship of the unashamed. I have the Holy Spirit power. The die has been cast. I have stepped over the line. The decision has been made—I'm a disciple of His. I won't look back, let up, slow down, back away, or be still. My past is redeemed, my present makes sense, my future is secure. I'm finished and done with low living, sight walking, smooth knees, colorless dreams, tamed visions, worldly talking, cheap giving, and dwarfed goals.
> >
> > I no longer need preeminence, prosperity, position, promotions, plaudits, or popularity. I don't have to be right, first, tops, recognized, praised, regarded, or rewarded. I now live by faith, lean in His presence, walk by patience, am uplifted by prayer, and I labor with power.
> >
> > My face is set, my gait is fast, my goal is heaven, my road is narrow, my way rough, my companions are few, my Guide reliable, my mission clear. I cannot be bought, compromised, detoured, lured away, turned back, deluded, or delayed. I will not flinch in the face of sacrifice, hesitate in the presence of the enemy, pander at the pool of popularity, or meander in the maze of mediocrity.
> >
> > I won't give up, shut up, let up, until I have stayed up, stored up, prayed up, paid up, preached up for the cause of Christ. I am a disciple of Jesus. I must go till He comes, give till I drop, preach till all know, and work till He stops me. And, when He comes for His own, He will have no problem recognizing me…my banner will be clear![a]
>
> a. Quoted from Brennan Manning's *The Signature of Jesus*; and Catherine Martin's *Pilgrimage of the Heart*.

of Redemption. He is calling you saying, "Follow Me!" Will you join us and answer His call?

The following chapters and appendixes will help you understand what we believe Scripture teaches us about discipleship and how we are to live it out. We claim now that this is not perfect. Only He who we follow is perfect. Our goal is to provide all our members with some beginning steps toward this goal. Remember, our journey in discipleship is usually not in leaps and bounds (although those may occur at times), but in small intentional steps taken daily for the love of Jesus Christ and the glory of God, the Father. These pages are filled with our journey of discovery. This journey has been taking place over many years, and we have learned many things (and will continue to do so). However, we believe that we can't tarry any longer and wait for something "perfect." Instead, we need to move forward, following the one who is perfect, and to trust that He will lead us on the path.

So we call you to join us in this journey. If you are satisfied with a Fast Food Christianity and being a member of the Club of Christ, then you may not like what we have to share. In fact, you will most likely complain and/or look for holes in the plan to keep from joining. However, if you are ready and are no longer satisfied with where you have been, but want to live fully in the life God has called you to, then keep reading, learning, growing, and living your journey of discipleship with us. Will you join us?

Before we move on, and before you make this commitment, I ask that you commit to being a part of the Fellowship of the Unashamed and that you pray the prayer of "A Disciple's Renewal." We want our journey together to start with a commitment to and with God. But be careful! When you make such a commitment and pray such a prayer, God expects that you will follow through. Don't make the commitment and pray the prayer if you don't mean the words.

Are you ready to make the commitment to true discipleship? Then let's start the journey...

Chapter 2

Two Truths—D²

We hold these truths to be self-evident! When the founding fathers of the United States wanted to be free from the tyranny and oppression of the British monarchy, they penned (on pain of death for treason) the Declaration of Independence. They were convicted that the colonies should separate from the rule and power of another to claim freedom for those who could not claim it for themselves. Through that conviction, they wrote the following:

> When in the Course of human events it becomes necessary for one people to dissolve the political bands which have connected them with another and to assume among the powers of the earth, the separate and equal station to which the Laws of Nature and of Nature's God entitle them, a decent respect to the opinions of mankind requires that they should declare the causes which impel them to the separation.

Why is this important? A ruling power exists in this world that we often ignore. In fact, this rule and authority is unseen. "For we do not wrestle against flesh and blood, but against the rulers, against the authorities, against the cosmic powers over the present darkness, against the spiritual forces of evil in the heavenly places" (Ephesians 6:12). It is an oppressive and tyrannical rule that seeks nothing else but to enslave all humanity.

Yet, this rule is deceptive and often promises every human desire, if one will just relinquish their soul. Take note, the ruler of this governing power is a tyrant. He cares nothing for those he rules over and wants nothing more than to devour them.[1] He cares for nothing or no one but himself. However, people are drawn to him as he deceives them and promises them great things. In fact, he blinds the eyes of people who do not believe so that they cannot see the light and glory of freedom found only through Jesus.[2] Instead, those individuals follow the course of the ruling authority in this world, the prince of the power of the air, who is at work in those of disobedience (who seek only to gratify the god of "self").[3]

The interesting thing is that we do not have to live under this rule. Like the freedom that is lived out in the United States, it has been bought with blood. But not by the blood of many, but by the blood of One. One who came to fight for us, to claim victory for us, and to pronounce for us freedom from the tyrannical rule of sin and its ruler, Satan. Jesus, our Victor, calls us to live a victorious life through Him. He asks us all to make a Declaration of Dependence upon Him—a declaration that may be confessed and lived on pain of death and suffering. A declaration that might state the following:

> When in the Course of the history of salvation, it becomes necessary for the unified people of God to dissolve the bonds of sin which have connected them with the world and separated them from God, a reverence to the redemption, bought by the blood of Christ, requires that they should declare the causes which urge them to the separation.

This Declaration of Dependence on Christ urges us toward truth that is found only in Jesus. As our founding fathers declared certain truths to be self-evident, today we hold this truth to be self-evident: Jesus is THE WAY, THE TRUTH, and THE LIGHT. No one can go to the Father except through Him.[4] This truth leads us to recognize two additional, irrefutable, self-evident truths regarding every human

---

1. 1 Peter 5:8.
2. 2 Corinthians 4:4.
3. Ephesians 2:2.
4. John 14:6.

being: (1) we are always being discipled and (2) we are always discipling someone.

We always have someone (or even something) influencing us toward a certain path in life. This influence can come through media (that may be discipling us toward self-fulfillment, self-worth, self-confidence); parents (who are discipling us toward success, achievement, and fulfillment); or friends (who may disciple us toward [fill in the blank]). The point is that we have individuals (or influencing messages, such as media, governments, philosophies, ideologies, and others) in our lives who are helping shape us into the people we are and will become. Those individuals are either led by the Spirit of God or by the spirit of the prince of this world. It is our job to discern which one.

The same can be said of the second point: We are always discipling someone. We may not be aware of that person and they may never let us know the influence we are having on their life, but we are nonetheless discipling them. We are making a direct impact on the way others live and the choices they make, for good (through the Spirit of God) or bad (through the spirit of the prince of this world). Each of us pulls from the available pool of resources (most of the time in way of relationships) to grow and to become the people we want to be.

The question then, is not an "if" but "who?" That is: (1) who (or even what) is discipling me and (2) whom am I discipling? The answers to those two questions help us discover the impact that others have on us and the impact we are having on them.

As Christians, having made the Declaration of Dependence on Christ, our desire is to follow our leader who calls us to fulfill the Great Commission in Matthew 28:18–20.

This was the mission of Christ, and therefore, it is our mission. If we accept Jesus' call to "follow me" and declare our state of dependence on Him, then we are called to live out His mission on earth as if He were living it through us. So, we must be diligent to know not only the words of the Great Commission, but also how to live them out. Through Jesus' words we discover four words of action: go, make, baptize, and teach (disciples). But what do the words mean for us?

Go and make. The Great Commission tells us to go and make disciples! That means that we must pursue the lost and help them in the process of becoming a disciple of Jesus. It means that we cannot grow

---

And Jesus came and said to them, "All authority in heaven and on earth has been given to me. Go therefore and make disciples of all nations, baptizing them in the name of the Father and of the Son and of the Holy Spirit, teaching them to observe all that I have commanded you. And behold, I am with you always, to the end of the age."

Matthew 28:18–20

comfortable in our pews, but are called to stand up and go out. Our job as disciples of Christ is to help the lost accept Jesus as their Lord and Savior and to prepare them to spread His Word and love to others. But *how* do we go and do this? The Great Commission tells us two ways.

Baptize. We have often confused baptism with being the Great Commission itself. Baptism is the *how*, not the *commission*. What is the purpose of baptism? Baptism allows us to personally participate in the gospel message: the death, burial, and resurrection of Jesus (Romans 6:3–8). Baptism is an expression of our faith in Jesus and identifies us as believers with the person and work of Jesus Christ (Galatians 3:26–27). At baptism, we receive the forgiveness of sins and the gift of the Holy Spirit (Acts 2:38).

Now, some will argue those points. However, at FXCC we believe that Scripture indicates that baptism fulfills these things. A question that usually arises, "Is baptism necessary for salvation?" The best response we have is this: salvation belongs to our God. When and how it happens is up to Him. We simply want to be faithful to His commands. However, baptism *is necessary for discipleship*. Why? Because Jesus said so. If you don't believe this, then read the Great Commission again. But, here's the deal. We are not done in discipling others when they repent of their sins, confess and accept Christ Jesus as their Lord and Savior, and are baptized into Christ. No, the journey is actually just beginning. Our role in discipleship continues and the Great Commission tells us how.

Teach. To simply baptize someone leaves the job of discipling only partially done. The second *how* to the Great Commission is to *teach*. We must teach those we baptize what the *commitment* of discipleship means. To teach means to equip believers to be active in their faith through serving God. But what does it mean to equip others? The online Merriam-Webster dictionary gives the following definitions: "to furnish for service or action by appropriate provisioning, to make ready: PREPARE." If this is true, then how do we equip new disciples of Christ? We can do so in three ways:

1. Teach them that being a Christian is an everyday commitment (Matthew 16:24; Mark 8:34; Luke 9:23, 14:26–27, 14:33).
2. Teach them that part of that commitment to Christ is a commitment to His body (church/family). That means they must be an

active participant in the family (1 Corinthians 12:12–13; Ephesians 2:19–22, 4:1–16).
3. Teach them the necessary skills for spreading God's love (that is, relationships, knowledge of God's Word, love, and others).

Those four words of action will push us toward fulfilling the Great Commission. While understanding the definitions helps us understand the action we need to take, they can often leave us wondering what is at the core of Christ's mission. Our mission for discipleship needs to be clear so that every person at Fairfax Church of Christ will work together toward a common purpose. This brings us to our shared mission for discipleship at Fairfax.

Our Mission for Discipleship

Today, there is a great deal of discussion about discipleship and spiritual formation. There are many differing opinions about what it is and how to define it. At Fairfax, we have spent a great deal of time in prayer, fasting, and study to seek the Lord and what He says concerning His call to make disciples and how that impacts His body here. It should be said that we align ourselves with no special group of individuals who have made claims concerning discipleship and spiritual formation. Instead, we recognized the inevitability of discipleship and spiritual formation for those who declared their dependence on Jesus and who truly desire to love and seek Him daily. So, we decided to be intentional about our efforts to foster spiritual growth that leads one toward transformation into the image of Christ.

Our mission is God's mission! It is our desire to do all we can (through God's power and the leading of His Spirit) to ensure that the family of God at Fairfax seeks to *make devoted followers of Jesus Christ who passionately lead others to Him* (both on an individual level and as a collective whole). In fact, this is the mission for all God's people. C.S. Lewis puts it this way:

> Every Christian is to become a **LITTLE CHRIST**. The whole purpose of becoming a Christian is simply nothing else…. In the same way the Church exists for nothing else but to draw men into Christ, to make them **LITTLE**

Discipling Others — D^2 — **Being Discipled**

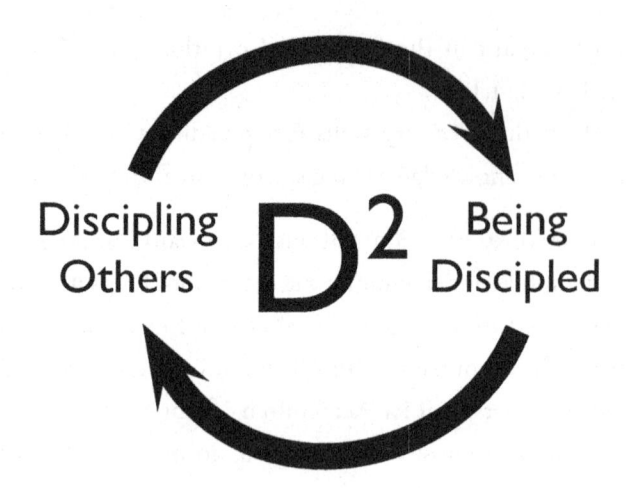

CHRISTS. If they are not doing that, all the cathedrals, clergy, missions, sermons, even the Bible itself, are simply a waste of time. God became Man for no other purpose.[5]

So, on an individual level, our goal is to *become a disciple who makes disciples*. But as a church family, we want to *make disciples who make disciples* or what we call D^2 (see graphic).

With this in mind, we seek to allow God's Spirit and His Word to infiltrate all areas of life and ministry as a guide and filter toward becoming devoted followers (disciples) of Jesus Christ. We recognize that as humans we will often fail at this, but we trust in God and His ability to lead us in these efforts. Like Paul said to the Colossians, we toil and struggle with the energy and power of Christ within us "that we may present everyone mature in Christ" and "that you may stand mature, and fully assured in all the will of God" (Colossians 1:28 and 4:12).

We only wish that He alone may receive all glory and honor and that we (as a family) are recognized simply as His children who love and follow Him as we live out His mission on earth.

In the coming chapters, you will find information concerning how we live out our Declaration of Dependence on Christ and God's

---

5. C.S. Lewis, *Mere Christianity* (HarperCollins, eBook), 177, 199 (emphasis added).

mission for discipleship at Fairfax (as we believe our Lord revealed it to us). We are confident of His revelation and recognize that He may continue to adapt it as He grows us and leads us ever closer to Him. In the following pages, we will look at how to be a disciple and how to disciple others so that they may all become more like Jesus (little Christs) every day. More specifically, we will discover how we plan to do this together as the family of God at Fairfax.

Chapter 3

Huh? What Does That Mean?

We began our journey in discipleship and spiritual formation through prayers, studies, and discussions asking, "What is Spiritual Maturity?" "What is a disciple?" "What is discipleship or discipling?" "What is spiritual growth or formation?" There are many differing answers to those questions. While others may disagree with the following answers and definitions, these will be the definitions we use as our frame of reference at Fairfax.

What is Spiritual Maturity?

We began our journey by asking the question, "What is **Spiritual Maturity**?" We spent weeks studying the different passages in the Bible that speak to it (see sidebars).

They were but a few of the passages we found that spoke to spiritual maturity. Through them, we discovered that spiritual maturity is attained as we grow in the knowledge of God's Word. Yet, it is more than simple knowledge, but a practical living out of the knowledge of God's Word in everyday life. It is *being the living Word of God*. From those passages, we determined that spiritual maturity is *an ever-increasing ability to apply God's Word to life*.

> And he gave the apostles, the prophets, the evangelists, the shepherds and teachers, to equip the saints for the work of ministry, for building up the body of Christ, until we all attain to the unity of the faith and of the knowledge of the Son of God, to mature manhood, to the measure of the stature of the fullness of Christ, so that we may no longer be children, tossed to and fro by the waves and carried about by every wind of doctrine, by human cunning, by craftiness in deceitful schemes. Rather, speaking the truth in love, we are to grow up in every way into him who is the head, into Christ, from whom the whole body, joined and held together by every joint with which it is equipped, when each part is working properly, makes the body grow so that it builds itself up in love.
>
> Ephesians 4:11-6

Note that we found it to be "ever-increasing." We will not have a full knowledge of God's Word in this life, but we should strive each day to know God more through His Word. The more we strive, the more we grow. The more we grow, the more we live out that knowledge daily for His glory and not our own. We believe that spiritual maturity is evident in an individual when one's faith

- Serves as the catalyst for how and why one thinks about things.
  - Creates the lens through which life is seen (2 Corinthians 4:18; Ephesians 1:17–23).
  - Motivates and shapes thinking (Romans 12:1–2; 1 Corinthians 2:10–16; Hebrews 3:1).
- Provides the means and focal point for "centering" oneself.
  - Gives certainty in an uncertain world, surety when life is anything but sure (Luke 1:3–4; John 17:8; Hebrews 11:1).
  - Provides the ability to weather life's storms and experience joy (Matthew 11:28–30; 2 Corinthians 4:7–12, 16–17).
- Defines one's interaction with others.
  - Encourages one to recognize and respond to needs (Galatians 6:10; Philippians 2:1–4; 1 John 3:18).
  - Motivates one to be supportive and to build up (Ephesians 4:11–16).
  - Means Christ-like behavior and attitude in our love, concern, care, and compassion (Ephesians 4:29–5:2).
  - Defines and shapes how one deals with the world (John 17:13–19; Romans 12:1–2).

We are all called, as disciples of Christ, to grow toward spiritual maturity. We are called to come to know God through His Word and to live that Word out each day.

What Is a Disciple?

When our studies led us to this conviction, we began to ask ourselves, "What is a **Disciple**?" We discovered many definitions floating out there as we studied. As we noted in the Introduction, there is a big difference in being a "convert" and being a "disciple" of Christ. We knew there was something more than being a Fast Food Christian who belonged to the Club of Christ.

As we dug, we found that a disciple is not satisfied with surface messages, surface relationships, or a surface life. They want to go deeper, know more, live more, and be known more by the one whom they follow. A disciple is an apprentice. Someone who decides to be *with* another person to learn to do what that person *does* or to become who that person *is*. But this comes into sharp contrast with worldly expectations that say you are your own person or individual. Yet, a disciple of Christ is someone who is learning from Christ how to live his or her life in the way Christ would live that life if He were that person. So, how would Christ live your life if He were living it?

A general (even worldly) definition of a disciple is "a committed follower of a great master." However, a more specific definition for Christians is "a disciple of Jesus is one who has come to Jesus for eternal life, has claimed Jesus as Savior and God, and has embarked upon the life of following Jesus."[1] So, a disciple *is one who demonstrates the ever-increasing characteristics of spiritual maturity as the Spirit of Christ dwells in one and is transforming one into His image.*

This is a very different picture than what we often think is required of us as Christians. After all, isn't it about Jesus saving us from our sins so that we can be in heaven? Yet, a life lived with that mindset and attitude is one that focuses on how salvation is for us, rather than how salvation is about Him. When we begin to truly grasp the depths of what God did for us through His Son, then we cannot help but desire to live a life that is in praise and thanksgiving to God for His gift and tremendous display of love.

However, we are often completely satisfied with receiving God's grace with little to no regard for giving it. We desire to gain all the privileges of a disciple minus the needed commitment to be one. But, we are asking all members at Fairfax to become true disciples of Jesus Christ. Not only in name, but also in life. To be a true disciple we must (1) come after Jesus, (2) deny ourselves, (3) take up our cross (suffering and rejection) daily, and then (4) Follow Him (Luke 9:23). We like to skip steps 1–3 and start at step 4 and say we are okay. But Jesus requires

---

1. Michael J. Wilkins, *Following the Master: Discipleship in the Steps of Jesus* (Grand Rapids: Zondervan, 1992), 40.

> Now I rejoice in my sufferings for your sake, and in my flesh I am filling up what is lacking in Christ's afflictions for the sake of his body, that is, the church, of which I became a minister according to the stewardship from God that was given to me for you, to make the word of God fully known, the mystery hidden for ages and generations but now revealed to his saints. To them God chose to make known how great among the Gentiles are the riches of the glory of this mystery, which is Christ in you, the hope of glory. Him we proclaim, warning everyone and teaching everyone with all wisdom, that we may present everyone mature in Christ. For this I toil, struggling with all his energy that he powerfully works within me.
>
> Colossians 1:24-29

> For though by this time you ought to be teachers, you need someone to teach you again the basic principles of the oracles of God. You need milk, not solid food, for everyone who lives on milk is unskilled in the word of righteousness, since he is a child. But solid food is for the mature, for those who have their powers of discernment trained by constant practice to distinguish good from evil. Therefore let us leave the elementary doctrine of Christ and go on to maturity, not laying again a foundation of repentance from dead works and of faith toward God, and of instruction about washings, the laying on of hands, the resurrection of the dead, and eternal judgment.
>
> Hebrews 5:12-6:2

that we start at step 1 and then proceed through to step 4. This is the ongoing process of growth as a disciple called *discipleship*.[2]

What Is Discipleship?

We all willingly enter this process of discipleship to become more like Jesus and live our lives as if He were living them for us. Yet, we wondered what is meant by the term "discipleship." The word "discipleship" is not found in the Bible, though it is addressed. We hear it all the time, but what is it? Well, know with certainty that it is not a program in the church or an offset ministry limited to those who are "gifted" for it. Discipleship is NOT a *ministry in the church*, it IS *the ministry of the church*. Bill Hull makes this point:

> Discipleship isn't a program or an event; it's a way of life. It's not for a limited time, but for our whole life. Discipleship isn't for beginners alone; it's for all believers for every day of their life. Discipleship isn't just one of the things the church does; it IS what the church does.[3]

Once we have become a disciple of Christ, then *discipleship is living as disciples or apprentices of Jesus Christ*. So, we define discipleship as Wilkins does. Discipleship is "the ongoing process of growth as a disciple."[4] Or, what we would call *the process of ever-increasing formation of Christ in our lives*. It involves making other disciples of Christ as Jesus is discipling us. This is called discipling. But to MAKE disciples we must BE disciples.

> And he said to all, "If anyone would come after me, let him deny himself and take up his cross daily and follow me."
>
> Luke 9:23

What Is Discipling?

Where Discipleship is the ongoing process of commitment and growth in Christ to become disciples, **discipling** is our part in aiding that commitment and growth in others. Remember D²?

---

2. Ibid.
3. Bill Hull, *The Complete Book of Discipleship: On Being and Making Followers of Christ* (Colorado Springs, CO: NavPress, 2006), 24.
4. Wilkins, Following the Master, 41.

First, we are becoming disciples, which is a life-long journey. But, the second part of D² is in discipling others while we are being discipled. As we make disciples, we call people to follow and imitate the growing *Christ in us* (not our self, in all its sinfulness). Perhaps that is why we often do not find ourselves discipling others. We are afraid!

- Afraid that we don't know enough.
- Afraid that our relationship with Christ isn't what it should be.
- Afraid to stick our noses into other people's lives as we are well aware of our own sinfulness.
- Afraid to call others to follow and imitate us because we are unsure if we are truly following Christ!

Yet, Paul was not afraid to call others to follow and imitate him and, in turn, disciple others in the same way. Please grab your Bible and study these very bold statements that Paul made:

- 1 Corinthians 4:14–17
- 1 Corinthians 11:1
- Philippians 3:17
- 2 Thessalonians 3:7
- 1 Timothy 4:12
- Titus 2:7–8

Having considered all of those passages, we agree with Wilkins' definition of discipling as "the responsibility of disciples helping one another to grow as disciples."[5] In other words, *this is our role and responsibility in helping others toward spiritual maturity*. Spiritual maturity only happens through the process of **Spiritual Formation** in our lives.

What Is Spiritual Formation?

You should remember here that in **discipleship** and **discipling**, we are simply joining the Holy Spirit in His work of **Spiritual Formation**:[6] *the process of being formed, conformed, and transformed into the*

---

5. Ibid.
6. Or what many term "spiritual growth."

image of Christ through the leading and guidance of the Holy Spirit. It is the role of the Holy Spirit to transform us into the image of Christ. Where discipleship is the ongoing process of becoming a disciple and discipling is our active role in that process to help others become disciples, **Spiritual Formation** is the Holy Spirit's role.

Consider spiritual formation in the way Paul shared it with the Corinthians:

> "I planted, Apollos watered, but God gave the growth. So neither he who plants nor he who waters is anything, but only God who gives the growth. He who plants and he who waters are one, and each will receive his wages according to his labor" (1 Corinthians 3:6–8).

According to this passage, one might understand seed planting as *evangelism* and watering as *discipleship/discipling*, but *spiritual formation* is God (through His Holy Spirit) causing the growth from the inside out.

Based on what we just shared, you might be wondering, "What about evangelism? What part does it play in all of this?" Those are great questions. Evangelism is *seed planting by the spreading of the Christian gospel through public preaching or personal witness*. It comes for the Greek word εὐαγγέλιον (euaggelion, pronounced *yoo-ang-ghel'-ee-on*), which means good news. Evangelism is *the spread of God's good news (Gospel) of salvation found only through Jesus Christ as expressed throughout the whole of Scripture*.

This is the first step of opening people up to the Gospel. They need to hear the word to receive it. As Paul writes to the Romans:

> For "everyone who calls on the name of the Lord will be saved." How then will they call on him in whom they have not believed? And how are they to believe in him of whom they have never heard? And how are they to hear without someone preaching? And how are they to preach unless they are sent? As it is written, "How beautiful are the feet of those who preach the good news!" But they have not all obeyed the gospel. For Isaiah says, "Lord, who has believed what he has heard from us?" So faith comes from hearing, and hearing through the word of Christ (Romans 10:13–17).

Evangelism is our role in spreading the good news of Jesus Christ so that people can call on the name of Jesus to be saved and to become His disciple. It is a crucial step. Yet, evangelism is a part of the discipleship process, not the whole. It is the beginning step in the overall process of discipleship. Unfortunately, we have often made evangelism the end. If we can bring them to the water, then we have done our job. But, it is only the beginning. True discipleship and discipling are carried out over a lifetime, not a moment. It is important that we keep this in mind as we move forward and grow.

So the answers to our questions and their subsequent definitions will now guide us through the following pages of our plan for discipleship at FXCC. By those definitions, we discover that our goal is to allow the Holy Spirit to use us to help others (and ourselves) move toward transformation into the image of Jesus. We must take an active role in the process as described to us in the Great Commission.

Chapter 4

Holy and Wholly Living "Do You Love Me?"

What do you love most? The answer to that question determines what someone makes his or her god. Whatever we love most is seen in where we spend most of our time, where we spend most of our resources, and whatever most of our thoughts and affections are directed toward. Since the beginning, God has wanted us to love Him more than anything else. Why? Because He knew that what we love most is our god. What we make our god is what we will draw from to make life decisions. Our god becomes the lens through which we see and interact with the world.

God is not satisfied with a part-time love relationship. The Shema in Deuteronomy 6:4–5 states,

> "Hear, O Israel: The LORD our God, the LORD is one. You shall love the LORD your God with all your heart and with all your soul and with all your might."

Jesus repeated those words when He was asked what the greatest command was:

> "The most important is, 'Hear, O Israel: The Lord our God, the Lord is one. And you shall love the Lord your God with all your heart and with all your soul and with all your mind and with all your strength.' The second is this:

'You shall love your neighbor as yourself.' There is no other commandment greater than these."[1]

Once God shared with His children that He alone was God, He wanted to make sure they knew how He wanted them to love Him: **holy** and **wholly**. This means that God *sets us apart* (**holy**) as His children and asks that we love Him not in part, *but in whole—heart, soul, mind, and strength* (**wholly**). God desires to have a deep and intimate relationship with His children because of His great love for us. He initiates this relationship with His children through His Spirit. The Holy Spirit connects with us through our soul and spirit (our inner core) and then infiltrates all other areas of our being.

Do You Love Me?

This is the **core of discipleship**! We are constantly being asked by God, "Do you *love* me?" This was Jesus' frame of reference when he restored Peter (after his denial of Jesus) in John 21:15–19, 22:

> When they had finished breakfast, Jesus said to Simon Peter, "Simon, son of John, do you love me more than these?" He said to him, "Yes, Lord; you know that I love you." He said to him, "Feed my lambs." He said to him a second time, "Simon, son of John, do you love me?" He said to him, "Yes, Lord; you know that I love you." He said to him, "Tend my sheep." He said to him the third time, "Simon, son of John, do you love me?" Peter was grieved because he said to him the third time, "Do you love me?" and he said to him, "Lord, you know everything; you know that I love you." Jesus said to him, "Feed my sheep. Truly, truly, I say to you, when you were young, you used to dress yourself and walk wherever you wanted, but when you are old, you will stretch out your hands, and another will dress you and carry you where you do not want to go." (This he said to show by what kind of death he was to glorify God.) And after saying this he said to him, "Follow me."[2]

---

1. Mark 12:29–31.
2. John 21:15–19.

Three times Jesus asks Peter, "Do you love me?" With each question, Jesus also has instructions. The instructions are Peter's means for demonstrating His love for Jesus. The instructions are also linked with Ezekiel 34 when God is rebuking the elders of His people. They have neglected their roles as shepherds and have instead fed themselves rather than God's children. So God says that He Himself will care for His flock. That HE will (1) *seek the lost*, (2) *bring back the strays*, (3) *bind up the injured*, and (4) *strengthen the weak* (Ezekiel 34:16).

God told the Israelites He would do this by setting up *one shepherd* over His people who would come from His servant David. He said through this *one shepherd* He would be with His flock and would be their God and His Shepherd would be among His people. Jesus fulfilled this role as our *one good shepherd*. He lived out seeking the lost, bringing back the strays, binding up the injured, and strengthening the weak. And when He was about to leave this earth, He instructed His disciples to live out His mission among His people.

The instructions He gives to Peter in John 21 are simply telling Him how to imitate the life that Jesus has already lived in fulfillment of Ezekiel 34. The instructions apply to us today as we seek to demonstrate our love for God. Consider His instructions in this way:

"Do we love Jesus more than _____ ("these," fill in the blank with your "these")? If so, then,

> **Feed my lambs** (seek the lost). Help the helpless by sharing God's love with those who do not know Him. Our role is to share the gospel message to the lost and helpless.
>
> **Tend my sheep** (bring back the strays and bind up the injured). Tend to the hurting children of God. Our walk of faith is difficult, and we must care for each other so that Satan does not get a foothold in any believer's life. We must guard against the attacks of Satan on the family of God.
>
> **Feed my sheep** (strengthen the weak). Feed the hungry. Those who hunger after God's Word and His love need constant feeding. As fellow children of God, we must be diligent with our soul feeding so that our love and attention are constantly directed back toward Jesus. When we are hungry and are not fed with the right food, we will find anything

> And he told them many things in parables, saying: "A sower went out to sow. And as he sowed, some seeds fell along the path, and the birds came and devoured them. Other seeds fell on rocky ground, where they did not have much soil, and immediately they sprang up, since they had no depth of soil, but when the sun rose they were scorched. And since they had no root, they withered away. Other seeds fell among thorns, and the thorns grew up and choked them. Other seeds fell on good soil and produced grain, some a hundredfold, some sixty, some thirty.
>
> Matthew 13:3–8

else that will provide us momentary sustenance. When we fail here, we begin to allow our brothers and sisters to become malnourished, and they will find themselves feeding on the refuse of the world.

Jesus provided those instructions and then said, "FOLLOW ME!"[3] To follow Jesus, we must come after Him, deny ourselves, take up our cross daily, and then follow Him.[4] Only then can we truly follow Jesus as His disciple.[5] Once we have accepted this relationship as a disciple, we begin to form spiritually as God has found "good soil" (Matthew 13:3–8; 18–23) that is receptive to His Word (both Jesus [the Word] and the written Word). He wishes to till and prepare that "good soil" so that it can grow and bear His good fruit. God tills and prepares this "good soil" in us through our heart, soul, mind, and strength.

Heart, Soul, Mind, and Strength

We could talk a lot about what exactly the heart, soul, mind, and strength of a man or woman are, and there is a great deal of discussion concerning their interpretations. But we want to focus on understanding that God intends for us to love Him with every bit of who we are. As humans, we recognize there are different aspects of our selves. What are these different aspects? Well, today we would understand them as

Heart. The heart represents our emotions (the seat of our love and affection). The Hebrew hearers would have understood heart (lēbhāb) to mean seat of intellect, will, and intention (and possibly emotions and feelings). As God has a passionate love for us, He in turn desires that we passionately love Him.[6]

---

3. John 21:19, 22.
4. Matthew 10:37–39; 16:24–26; Mark 8:34–38; Luke 9:23–24.
5. See pages 26–28 for more details.
6. Consider these passages concerning both the love of God from our heart and the stubbornness of our hearts toward God: Deuteronomy 4:29, 13:3, 26:16, 30:2, 30:6, and 30:10; Psalm 19:7, 25:1, 42:1, 62:1, 62:5, 63:1–8, 84:2, 130:5–6, and 143:5–8; Isaiah 26:9; Jeremiah 3:17, 9:14, 11:8, 13:10, 16:12, 18:12, and 23:17; Ezekiel 18:4; Matthew 10:28 and 16:24–26; and Romans 2:5.

Soul. The soul (nephesh) would have been understood to mean "being, life" and would have been understood in a broader sense to express "the whole inner self, with all the emotions, desires, and personal characteristics that make each human being unique."[7] Some believe that the pairing of heart and soul proposes "a distinction of some sort is being made between mental and emotional energy and activity."[8] For our understanding, the soul is understood as that moral or "spiritual center" part of us that "connects with God." Since we have "no other gods," our one and only God takes up residence in that center, and we meet with Him there through worship, prayer, spiritual disciplines, and other practices.[9]

Mind. Our mind is our intellect and thoughts. It is our ability to think rationally to reason, to process information, and to arrive at conclusions. We are to have the mind of Christ (Philippians 2:5).[10]

Strength. Strength or might (mě'ōd) is the physical side of each human with all its capacities and functions. The specific notion being used here is that of "muchness" and that Israel should love God with all of its essence and expression.[11] Some interpret might to mean our money and possessions while others believe that self-discipline is required so that God can be loved with all one's might.[12] So, our strength would be all we own as well as our behavior and how we put things into action. And we want our possessions and how we use them as well as our behavior and actions to reflect our heart (emotions), soul (moral and spiritual), and mind (thoughts and intellect).[13]

---

7. Wright, *Deuteronomy*, 99.

8. Christensen, *Deuteronomy*, 143.

9. Consider these passages concerning loving and obeying God with all our soul: Deuteronomy 4:29; 13:3; 26:16; 30:2, 6, 10; Psalm 19:7; 25:1; 42:1; 62:1, 5; 63:1–8; 84:2; 130:5–6; 143:5–8; Isaiah 26:9; Ezekiel 18:4; Matthew 10:28; 16:24–26.

10. Consider these passages concerning loving God with all of our mind: Romans 7:21–25; 8:5–8; 12:1–2; 1 Corinthians 14:13–17.

11. Merrill, *Deuteronomy*, 164.

12. Christensen, *Deuteronomy*, 143.

13. Consider these passages concerning loving God with all of our strength as we serve Him out of our love: Deuteronomy 10:12, 11:13; Joshua 22:5; James 2:14–26; 1 John 3:18; Colossians 3:17.

Our behavior and how we put things into action. It's our Service, Training, Modeling, and Mobilizing for Ministry and is reflective our inner Heart, Soul, and Mind.

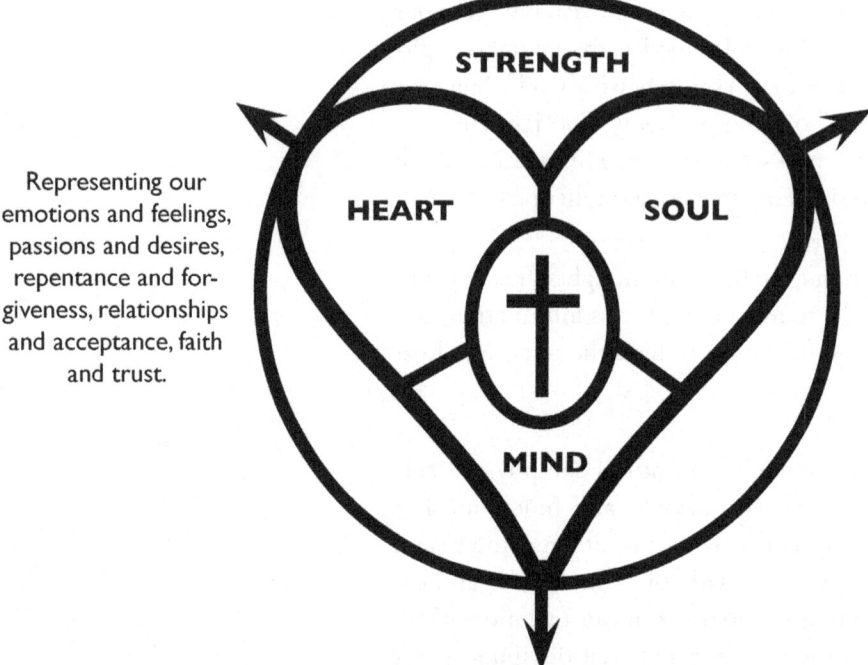

STRENGTH

HEART — Representing our emotions and feelings, passions and desires, repentance and forgiveness, relationships and acceptance, faith and trust.

SOUL — How we connect with God through worship, prayer, and spiritual disciplines as our spirit connects with God's Spirit.

MIND — Our intellect and thoughts; our ability to think rationally and to reason, process information, and arrive at conclusions concerning God's Word.

With all of that in mind, we cannot compartmentalize our love and devotion to God. He (and our love for Him) must encompass every aspect of our lives. Consider the visual in how we are to love God.

In the image, we recognize that the heart of a person is the core of who they are. In the heart is a hole. That hole may be filled with anything or anyone we choose. God placed that hole for a purpose. Ecclesiastes 3:11 (New International Version) says, "He has also set eternity in the human heart; yet no one can fathom what God has done from beginning to end." God intended that hole to be filled with

Him (eternity), yet humankind struggles with understanding it. So we often try to fill the hole with everything or everyone else but God. Yet, that hole is never filled. Only when God is set firmly in the hole in our hearts will we truly find fulfillment.

As you continue to look at the image, you discover that the heart (our inner self) has three aspects (yet is unified and whole). There is the **heart** (representing our feelings, passions, desires, forgiveness, etc.); the **soul** (how we connect with God through worship, prayer, and spiritual disciplines as we our spirit connects with the Spirit); and the **mind** (our intellect and thoughts; our ability to think rationally and to reason, process information, and arrive at conclusions). Those three aspects of our inner self work and function together to make us who we are. It is from our core that we act and behave, which is our **strength** (our possessions, behavior, and how we put things into action). We want our behavior and actions to reflect our heart (emotions), soul (moral and spiritual connection with God), and mind (thoughts and intellect).

If we fail to know and live this, we fail to know and live the very essence of Scripture and the very essence of who we are. The Israelites were commanded to place the commandments "upon their hearts." It's evident that God wanted His children to think on, meditate about, experience, and live out "these words" (the Shema).

PHASES OF SPIRITUAL FORMATION

Understanding those aspects, we can discover and discern some phases of spiritual formation. As we studied this, we discovered that others were finding similar phases of spiritual formation. You can look at Willow Creek's *Reveal*, Jim Putman's *DiscipleShift*,[14] and others to see similar phases or stages of spiritual growth. However, during our studies we found that our phases of spiritual growth closely mimic the phases of our physical growth. So we used common phrases from developmental psychology to differentiate what we believe to be the distinguishable phases of spiritual formation; what we call our "Spiritual Formation Continuum."

---

14. Please see Appendix A for reference information for *DiscipleShift*. Cally Parkinson and Greg L. Hawkins, *Reveal: Where Are You?* Barrington, IL: Willow Creek Association, 2007.

The Spiritual Formation Continuum

Spiritual Maturity
Someone whose Christianity has moved from a simple faith to a complex faith and back to a simple faith that honors God in every way. A "native speaker" of Christianity.

Spiritual Adulthood
Someone who is a Christian and has allowed themselves to be challenged in their faith. Therefore, they have grown through the process.

Spiritual Adolescence
Someone who has become a Christian and has been one for some time.

Spiritual Childhood
Someone in the stages of becoming a Christian by making commitment to Christ through baptism.

Spiritual Infancy
Someone who is not a Christian and has developing interest in this "Church thing" or God.

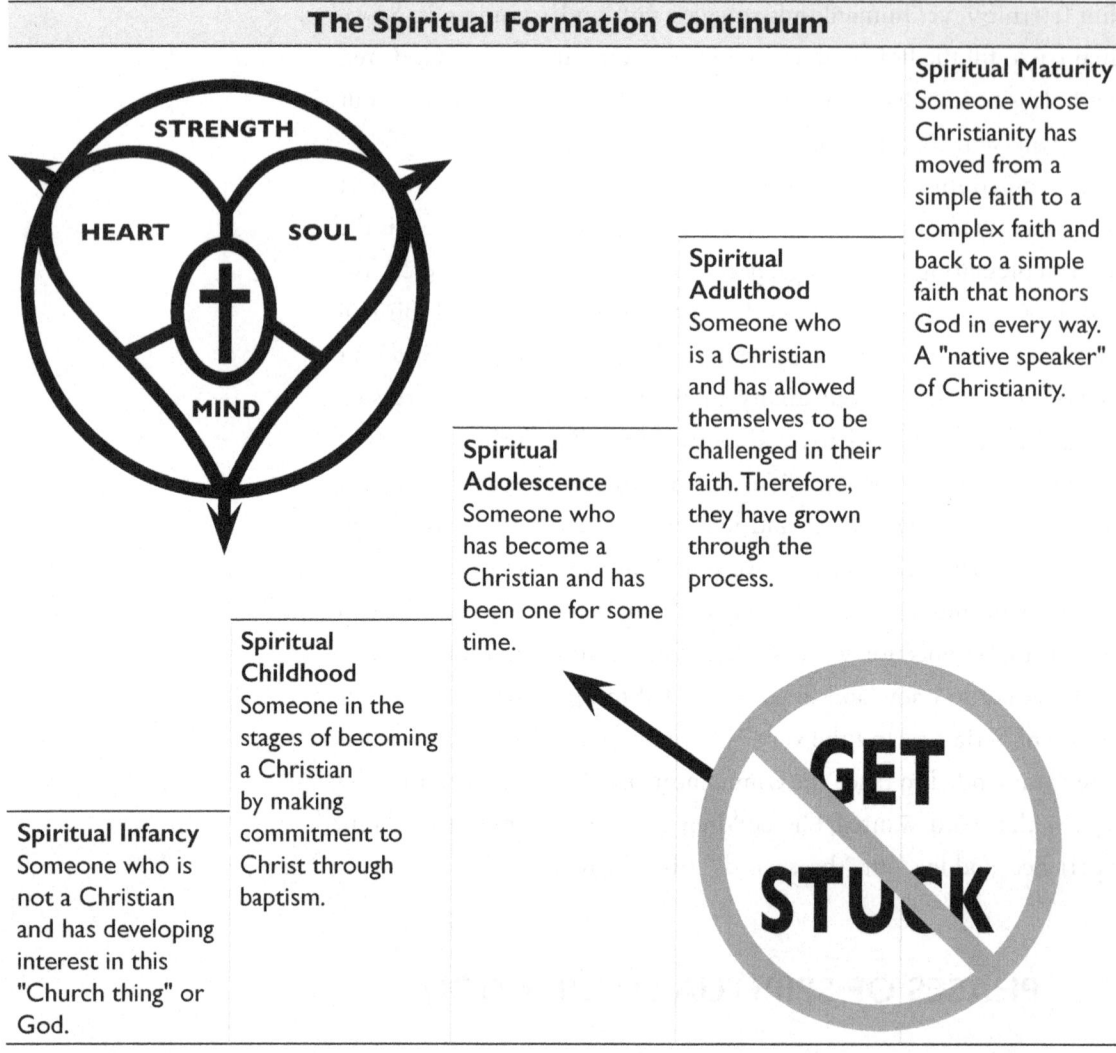

Note: Spiritual Maturity is evident in someone when their faith serves as the catalyst for how and why they think about things, provides the means and focal point for "centering" themselves, defines their interaction with others, and defines and shapes how they deal with the world.

Imagine the continuum as a set of stairs. Each phase of our lives moves us up those stairs toward a more intimate relationship with Christ as we continue to be transformed into His image. We must not "get stuck" on any one of those steps, but instead we must make every effort to move steadily up them. With each of the stages comes some sort of marker to indicate whether you are in any particular phase or have moved beyond it. The following are indicators that you are in a particular phase. Please remember, these indicators are dynamic, not static. We will often move up and down the stairs as we grow and encounter things in our lives. So you may exhibit indicators from a phase above or below. That does not mean you are stuck, but may indicate an area of needed growth.

Indicators for Each Spiritual Phase

Spiritual Infancy

Someone who is not a Christian and has a developing interest in this "church thing" or God.

Heart

- Is heavily influenced by the world
- Lacks trust in relationships
- Struggles with feelings of acceptance ("Can I come? Do you mean me, too?")
- Questions whether forgiveness is possible

Soul

- Has an inherited or passed-down faith
- Seeks God through prayer or Bible reading only when in need (Is there a God and who is this Jesus? What does Jesus mean to me?)

Mind

- Has little to no biblical knowledge
- Has little understanding of moral absolutes
- Learns one-on-one with a minister or close personal friend

Strength

- Has little to no practice of faith

Needs

- Worship: Observer
- Develop relationships through—
  - Orientation classes

- o   Bible classes
- o   Growth groups (for connection purposes)
- o   Gender specific activities (men's breakfast, women's Bible class, others)
- o   Service opportunities

Spiritual Childhood

Someone in the stages of becoming a Christian by making a commitment to Christ through baptism.

Heart

- Is in beginning stage of trust in God and His people (need for relationships)
- Knows forgiveness is possible, but is still questioned

Soul

- Understands faith is taught versus owned (for example, "I heard a Brother say…" versus "I believe…")
- Makes time sporadically for personal Bible reading and prayer

Mind

- Has exposure to basic Biblical principles that builds a framework (rule set) that guides thinking and development
- Learns through Sunday morning sermons

Strength

- Understands the need to serve, but self will take precedence over service

Needs

- Worship: From Observer to Participant (24/7)
- Begin practicing "Acts of Righteousness"
  - o   Personal study of God's Word

- o Silence, solitude, meditation
- o Prayer
- o Giving
- o Fasting
- o Others
- Deepen relationships through
  - o Bible classes
  - o Growth groups (for depth)
  - o Gender specific activities (men's breakfast, women's Bible class, others)
  - o Service opportunities

Spiritual Adolescence
(a stage where some often get stuck)

Someone who has become a Christian and has been one for some time.

Heart

- Begins to find a place and knows what one can do in the midst of community (at Fairfax) by recognizing one's own Spiritual gifts and how they can be used
- Feels forgiven and accepted in the Church

Soul

- Begins to see oneself in the story of faith rather than just know the story of faith
- Sees growth as one moves from a faith based on external direction or motivation to one that is grounded in a unique identity found only in Christ
  - o Needs to move from an inherited or obligated faith to a faith built on convictions
- Makes time for personal Bible reading and prayer most days

Mind

- Connects Biblical principles to practice in daily life

- Begins to ask "What do I believe and why?" for a deeper understanding of the link between Biblical principles and practice
- Learns in Bible classes and growth groups

Strength

- Feels obligated to serve and share faith (though this occurs infrequently)

Needs

- Worship: From Participant to Contributor
- Discover Spiritual gifts through assessment and mentoring (for feedback)
- Begin involvement in ministry
- Help teach a Bible class
- Practice of "Acts of Righteousness" becomes a habit
    - Personal study of God's Word
    - Silence, solitude, meditation
    - Prayer
    - Giving
    - Fasting
    - Others
- Deepen relationships through
    - Mentoring
    - Accountability group

Spiritual Adulthood

Someone who is a Christian and has allowed themselves to be challenged in their faith. Therefore, they have grown through this process.

Heart

- Tends to look beyond oneself to the care, love, and nurture of others

Soul

- Begins to enjoy daily communion with God through prayer, study, worship, and other practices (that has become reflective, thoughtful,

contemplative) as a daily practice of living God's grace that informs every act, word, or thought
- Lives the process of building a liberating faith rather than a restrictive one
- Reaches the crisis of re-entrenching to a more simplistic form of faith (Spiritual Adolescence or earlier) or one that is thoughtful and discipleship oriented

Mind

- Has a foundation firm enough to discuss biblically prescribed issues while being able to differentiate prescribed from traditional practices
- Has challenges in the formation of a thoughtful simplicity (that is, the ability to reflect on complex issues yet find the peace that comes with simplicity)

Strength

- Learns through practice as one finds oneself teaching, leading service projects, becoming a ministry leader, mentoring others, and others

Needs

- Worship: From Contributor to Initiator
- Initiate ministries
- Initiate worship opportunities
- Initiate a Bible class or study
- Initiate a growth group
- Practice "Acts of Righteousness" daily and help others through mentoring
    - Personal study of God's Word
    - Silence, solitude, meditation
    - Prayer
    - Giving
    - Fasting
    - Others
- Initiate relationships through
    - Mentoring others

- o   Growth group
- o   Accountability group
- o   Service opportunities

Spiritual Maturity

Someone whose Christianity has moved from a simple faith to a complex faith and back to a simple faith that honors God in every way. A "native speaker" of Christianity.

Heart

- Desires what God desires, implying that one's emotional life has been transformed and formed
- Surrenders to Jesus as Lord and reveals that surrendering through ones actions (self-surrender is central to this stage)
- Has faith marked by a trust, confidence, and hope in God that has developed over time

Soul

- Owns faith that can be explained and shared
- Breathes personal Bible reading and prayer—it just happens!

Mind

- Has self-directed learning
- Augments knowledge and study (history, evolution of doctrine, comparative studies, and others)
- Completes deeper, more nuanced studies in scripture and application to life

Strength

- Moves beyond believing and acting "correctly" to practicing from Christian motives
- Shares belief and knowledge in growth groups and personal mentoring

- Shares God's grace naturally and obviously in daily life (the journey is not complete, but only beginning)

The journey moves how we see God and our walk with Him from
SIMPLE ➡ COMPLEX ➡ SIMPLE

Needs

- Worship: From Initiator to Imitator
- You cannot *not*
    - Love Jesus
    - Love Others
    - Share Jesus
    - Serve Jesus
    - Serve Others
- "Acts of Righteousness" are breath (one *must* breathe in God's Word, talk with Him unceasingly) and *must* be shared (Jeremiah 20:9)
    - Personal study of God's Word
    - Silence, solitude, meditation
    - Prayer
    - Giving
    - Fasting
    - Others
- Relationships through
    - Ongoing mentoring relationships
    - Some relationships have moved from mentoring to apprenticeship
    - Others seek your counsel
    - Others join you in what you are already doing (they want to imitate you because you imitate Him)

So, where are you? As you consider each of those phases and indicators, where do you fall in the continuum of spiritual formation? It's important to regularly assess your stage and even have others assess where they think you are. This assessment allows for a time of both introspection and discovering how others see your walk with Christ. Both are helpful toward continued growth rather than allowing yourself to get stuck. Therefore, some possible questions you can ask as you assess yourself and others are the following:

1. What are you doing to intentionally till and prepare the soil of your heart (emotional-self) so you may form a healthy relationship with God and others?
2. What are you doing to intentionally till and prepare the soil of your soul (spirit) so you may be receptive to God?
3. What are you doing to intentionally till and prepare the soil of your mind (thoughts, intellect), with the renewing of the mind, so that you can think and reason according to the Scriptures?
4. What are you doing to intentionally till and prepare the soil of your strength (faith and love in action) so that you are prepared for works of service and evangelism to build up the family of God?

The answer to those questions will help you discover what phase you are in or what phase others say you are in. You can then begin to form a plan of how you would like to grow and move further toward spiritual maturity. Look inward and allow others to share with you what they see in you. We pray this will be a blessing and will motivate you to move forward while you encourage others to do so. May God bless you in this!

Chapter 5

What Does a Disciple Look Like?

What does a disciple look like? Have you seen one lately? What distinguished him or her from everyone else? Often we (the Discipleship Team) have people ask us to share with them evidence of someone being a disciple of Christ. At first, we found ourselves struggling to put it down in words. We were convinced we knew what a disciple of Christ looked like, but we didn't know quite how to express it in words. Well, like anything else, it took us examining God's Word to discover the description, or profile, of a disciple of Jesus Christ.

A Biblical Profile of a Disciple of Christ

Based on everything we studied and discovered in the preceding pages, and after looking deeper into passages about disciples in Scripture, we found the following to be the best biblical descriptions of a disciple of Christ (one who truly follows Jesus). We hope this will provide you with motivation to grow in Christ and become more like Him every day.

1. **A Disciple is Committed**. A disciple of Christ is someone who has devoted his or herself to the Lordship of Jesus. He or she denies self and puts Christ first in every aspect of life. This is an eternal

commitment. (Matthew 6:9–13, 24, 33; Luke 9:23; John 13:13; 2 Corinthians 5:15)

2. **A Disciple is Obedient**. A disciple is committed to a life of submission to Christ. A disciple surrenders his or her life to God and continually says, "yes," to what God asks. (Deuteronomy 13:3–4; 1 Corinthians 6:19–20; Ephesians 4:22–5:5; 1 John 5:1–5)
3. **A Disciple is a Life-Long Learner**. A disciple of Christ is open to the leading of the Holy Spirit and is teachable. He or she is not a "know it all," but is instead growing spiritually over a lifetime. (Proverbs 9:8–10; Matthew 4:19; John 6:60–66)
4. **A Disciple is a Fruit Bearer**. A disciple practices spirituality to be transformed by the Holy Spirit and demonstrate the fruit of the Spirit in his or her life. (Galatians 5:22–23)
5. **A Disciple is Devoted to prayer and practices**. A disciple spends time in daily devotion and is constantly developing his or her prayer life. (Psalm 27:4, 42:1–2; Mark 1:35; Luke 11:1–4)
6. **A Disciple is Shaped by the Word**. A disciple longs to learn and apply the Word of God to his or her life. One does this through hearing the Word preached and taught, reading the Bible regularly, going to group Bible studies, memorizing Scripture, and meditating on the Scriptures. (John 8:31; Acts 17:11; Colossians 3:16; 2 Timothy 2:15)
7. **A Disciple is a Servant**. A disciple is God's servant who actively engages in helping others in practical ways. (Act 6:1–4)
8. **A Disciple is a Witness**. A disciple wants to be a witness for God and share His message of salvation. A disciple intentionally presents the Gospel regularly with increasing skill. (Matthew 28:18–20; Acts 1:8; Romans 1:16; 1 Thessalonians 2:4)
9. **A Disciple is a Cheerful Giver**. A disciple honors God through his or her time, possessions, and finances. (1 Corinthians 16:1–2; 2 Corinthians 9:7)
10. **A Disciple is Faithful**. A disciple faithfully meets and fellowships with other members of God's family (through church services, Bible studies, discipleship groups, prayer groups). In those contexts, his or her spiritual needs are met and, in turn, can make a contribution to the body of Christ. (Psalm 122:1; Acts 16:5; 1 Corinthians 12:12–27; Hebrews 10:24–25; 1 John 1:3)

Expectations of Disciples at FXCC

As we looked over this Biblical profile of a disciple of Christ, we began to ask ourselves if it points us to expectations of what it means to be a disciple of Christ as a part of the family of God at Fairfax Church of Christ. We kept the following question in front of us to see what God would lead us to do.

What does it mean to be a disciple of Christ at Fairfax Church of Christ?

In any family, there is a set of expectations that family members observe (whether spoken or often unspoken). The expectations guide how the relationships between family members work. In church families, expectations are often not discussed and are shied away from. We are afraid that in sharing them we will run people off.

Expectations for involvement in team sports, civic and volunteer organizations, school, and other activities are well known and placed on every member of society. Yet, the work of the Lord's church carries much more weight than any of those worldly pursuits. We believe that the lack of impact for Christ in our nation (and perhaps the world) is evident because there are little to no expectations placed on church members. As we see in the New Testament, members of the Lord's family must be committed to ministry through their local church (fellowship, family).

Based on all our discussions in the preceding pages on discipleship at FXCC, we do not want to shy away from expectations as disciples of Christ. Instead, we would like each member to understand how our family works and what is expected of each family member. We desire each member to be an active participant in the kingdom work that is going on here at this church. The following is our best attempt to be faithful to what Scripture outlines as "family expectations" in the Lord's church.

1. **I will believe.** I believe that Jesus Christ is the Son of God. I believe that He died on a cross to set me free from sin. I believe that He rose from the grave with the promise to raise me from the

grave (both physical and spiritual) to live with Him for eternity in heaven. (Mark 16:16; John 11:25–26, 20:29, 20:31; Acts 16:31; Romans 5:1–2; 10:4, 10:9–11; 1 Corinthians 15:3–11)

2. **I will commit.** I will commit my life to Christ and become His disciple (follower or apprentice of Jesus). I understand that part of my commitment is to repent of my past life of sin, to confess Jesus as my Lord and Savior, and to be baptized into His name and thus added to His family. (If you have any questions about God's plan of salvation, please don't hesitate to ask. We will be happy to explain what we believe the Bible teaches on the subject. Ultimately, it is your decision.) (*Repent*—Luke 24:45–47; Acts 3:19, 17:30; 2 Peter 3:9) (*Confess*—Matthew 10:32; Romans 10:9–13; Philippians 2:11; 1 John 4:15) (*Baptism*—Acts 2:38; Romans 6:1–7; Galatians 3:27; Colossians 2:12; 1 Peter 3:21)

3. **I will worship.** I understand that being a member of the Lord's church means that I will meet regularly with other members of God's family to worship Him with all my heart, soul, mind, and strength in Spirit and in truth. (2 Kings 17:28–39; Psalms 29:2, 95:6, 99:5, 99:9, 100:2; Matthew 4:10; John 4:20–24; Romans 12:1; Hebrews 12:28; Revelation 7:11, 14:7, 22:8–9)

4. **I will grow.** I understand that part of my commitment to Christ is to grow spiritually as His disciple. I know that growth takes place not only individually, but also with other brothers and sisters in Christ. So, I will work to foster my spiritual growth through Bible studies, a growth group, spiritual disciplines, and any other means that may help me grow and be transformed into the image of Christ. (Ephesians 4:11–16; Philippians 1:6, 3:12–15; Colossians 1:9–10; 2 Timothy 3:16–17; Hebrews 5:12–14, 6:1–2; 1 Peter 2:1–3; 2 Peter 3:17–18)

5. **I will serve.** Like Christ, I understand that I did not become a disciple of Christ to be served, but to serve others and to give my life for the sake of Christ. I recognize that I am a part of the body of Christ and have been given gifts by the Holy Spirit for the purpose of building up the body of Christ and those in need. I understand that to serve is to sacrifice. To sacrifice is to give up what may be best for me for the good of others and for the glory of God. Therefore, I will work each day to be a living sacrifice to God. (Acts 2:45;

1 Corinthians 9:19; 2 Corinthians 9:6–15; Galatians 5:13; 1 Peter 4:8–11)

6. **I will share.** I commit to living out the Great Commission by going out and sharing my faith to those who do not know the Lord. I want to share the love and grace of God (given through Christ) that has been freely given to me so that others may know and share in it with me. (Matthew 28:18–20; Mark 16:15–16; Acts 4:18–20, 5:27–32, 5:40–42)

7. **I will give.** I understand that God loves a cheerful, generous spirit. I know that in giving to the family at Fairfax Church of Christ, I am giving to the work of God by giving my time, talents, and treasures. I know that all I have is His and that giving back to Him is just a small portion of what He has given me. I understand that through giving, I am helping fund and promote ministries and missions that support the expansion of God's kingdom and help those in need. (Matthew 6:1–4; 2 Corinthians 8:1–15, 9:6–15)

8. **I will seek unity.** I understand that others will know I am a Christian by how I love my brothers and sisters in Christ. Therefore, I will seek to bring unity rather than division in our family at FXCC. I commit to seeking out my brother or sister when I know I have wronged them or I know they have sinned against me. I will model the reconciliation of God to those around me by loving others as Christ has loved me. (John 13:34–35, 15:12, 17:20–23; 1 Corinthians 1:10; Colossians 3:12–14)

9. **I will pray.** I know that God listens to me and longs for me to talk with Him. So I will commit to being a person of prayer. I will regularly kneel before my God on behalf of others and myself and will seek to grow in my relationship with God through continual conversations with Him. (Matthew 6:5–15; Luke 11:1–13, 18:1, 21:36; Romans 12:12; Ephesians 6:18; Colossians 4:2; 1 Thessalonians 5:17)

- **I will honor and respect.** I understand and respect the commitments outlined in the FXCC "What Our Family Believes" statements.[1] I also recognize and know the Vision, Mission, and Values

---

1. See Appendix E.

of FXCC[2] and commit to honoring the direction that God and my spiritual leaders at FXCC have laid out before me. I understand that as a member, I put myself under the oversight of the elders and will work to honor them as my spiritual leaders as they commit to shepherd me in my walk with Christ. (Acts 20:28; Philippians 1:1; 1 Timothy 3:1–7; Titus 1:5–9; 1 Peter 5:1–4)

We hope those family expectations demonstrate our desire to honor God and His will and purpose for our lives as His disciples. We hope they demonstrate the deep love we have for God and His people and how we want to intentionally live out His mission in our lives. We hope this will be a church family in which you too can use your God-given gifts in faithful, humble service to Him as you commit to fulfill these expectations for the glory of God. Will you join us in fulfilling these commitments?

---

2. See Appendix F.

Chapter 6

Developing a Plan for Spiritual Growth

We have learned a great deal about what it truly means to be a disciple of Christ. We now know that it is all encompassing and requires vigilance on our part to continue to grow more and more into the image of Christ. To continue in our growth in Christ, we must make plans toward that end. Think about it this way. Anything important in your life has required planning. Now, everyone's personality is a little different on how they plan, but they plan nonetheless. You could pick anything big that happens in your life: weddings, graduations, going to college, or moving. Each of those requires a great deal of planning toward accomplishing a particular goal. Let's choose going to college for a moment.

A student who wants to succeed in a particular field to gain employment in that area will spend a great deal of time looking at the different colleges that offer degrees in that field. From there, a student will begin to see which colleges offer the best options (that is, financial aid, location, well-known and respected teachers in the field, student-to-teacher ratios, length of program, grading scales, job placement after graduation percentages, and so on). Once the student has narrowed down the field of choices, he or she then might go and visit the campuses of the universities, meet with faculty, sit in classes, and visit the dorms. All this to simply choose the college the student believes will help him or her achieve the vocational goals in life. Why would we not spend as much time planning our growth in the most important aspect of our lives—our relationship with Christ?

Jesus taught His disciples the principle of planning when he discussed with them the need to count the cost of discipleship:

> Now great crowds accompanied him, and he turned and said to them, "If anyone comes to me and does not hate his own father and mother and wife and children and brothers and sisters, yes, and even his own life, he cannot be my disciple. Whoever does not bear his own cross and come after me cannot be my disciple. *For which of you, desiring to build a tower, does not first sit down and count the cost, whether he has enough to complete it?* Otherwise, when he has laid a foundation and is not able to finish, all who see it begin to mock him, saying, 'This man began to build and was not able to finish.' *Or what king, going out to encounter another king in war, will not sit down first and deliberate whether he is able with ten thousand to meet him who comes against him with twenty thousand?* And if not, while the other is yet a great way off, he sends a delegation and asks for terms of peace. So therefore, any one of you who does not renounce all that he has cannot be my disciple.[1]

In that passage, Jesus not only prompts His disciples to count the cost of following Him, but also to plan for it. The moment we commit our lives to Christ we have joined Him in a lifelong journey toward being transformed into His image. We are journeying with Jesus through His Spirit toward Christlikeness from the point of our acceptance and commitment to Him until the day of our death or His return. If we believe that to be true, then we must not take the trip without making plans for the journey. This journey requires us to examine ourselves and to consider our walk with Him. Consider the following passages:

- Psalm 26:2-3: Prove me, O LORD, and try me; test my heart and my mind. For your steadfast love is before my eyes, and I walk in your faithfulness.
- Psalm 139:23-24: Search me, O God, and know my heart! Try me and know my thoughts! And see if there be any grievous way in me, and lead me in the way everlasting!

---

1. Luke 14:25–33 (emphasis added).

- Lamentations 3:40: Let us test and examine our ways, and return to the LORD!
- Haggai 1:5: Now, therefore, thus says the LORD of hosts: Consider your ways.
- 2 Corinthians 13:5: Examine yourselves, to see whether you are in the faith. Test yourselves. Or do you not realize this about yourselves, that Jesus Christ is in you?—unless indeed you fail to meet the test!
- Galatians 6:4: But let each one test his own work, and then his reason to boast will be in himself alone and not in his neighbor.
- Ephesians 5:15: Look carefully then how you walk, not as unwise but as wise…

Each of those passages (and others like them) attests to the need for us to continually examine our walk with Christ. Why? In order that we can know if we are walking in His way or not. This self-examination should motivate us to continually assess our current place on the map of discipleship so that we can make plans for continued growth. Solomon understood not only planning one's course, but relying on God as the guide. Meditate on the following passages (especially those portions that have been highlighted) from Proverbs:

- Proverbs 3:3-7: Let not steadfast love and faithfulness forsake you; bind them around your neck; write them on the tablet of your heart. So you will find favor and good success in the sight of God and man. *Trust in the LORD with all your heart, and do not lean on your own understanding. In all your ways acknowledge him, and he will make straight your paths.* Be not wise in your own eyes; fear the LORD, and turn away from evil.
- Proverbs 16:1-9: *The plans of the heart belong to man, but the answer of the tongue is from the LORD.* All the ways of a man are pure in his own eyes, but the LORD weighs the spirit. *Commit your work to the LORD, and your plans will be established.* The LORD has made everything for its purpose, even the wicked for the day of trouble. Everyone who is arrogant in heart is an abomination to the LORD; be assured, he will not go unpunished. By steadfast love and faithfulness iniquity is atoned for, and by the fear of the LORD one turns away from evil. When a man's ways please the LORD,

he makes even his enemies to be at peace with him. Better is a little with righteousness than great revenues with injustice. *The heart of man plans his way, but the LORD establishes his steps.*
- Proverbs 19:21: *Many are the plans in the mind of a man, but it is the purpose of the LORD that will stand.*

It is evident from those passages that God's desire for us is to make plans for our lives that are consistent with and in accordance with His will for our lives. He wants us to move through life with Him. So, if we truly want to be His disciples, then we must make plans in our lives that lead us down the path toward Him—that compels us to trust in Him as our God and guide, knowing He knows best and has a plan to lead us closer and closer to Him *that will stand.*

This is the same mindset Jesus had when telling His disciples not to worry about the needs of this life. Why? Our Father who loves us will provide for them.[2] Instead, our plans in life should be in seeking first the kingdom of God and His righteousness.[3] God will be faithful to those who are faithful to Him. What a wonderful God we love and serve! So, let's make some plans....

Making a Plan for Spiritual Growth

The purpose of a Plan for Spiritual Growth is to deliberately map your path for continued growth in Jesus. The plan can help you discover what steps you need to take to grow. Here are the customary elements of a plan for spiritual growth that could be incorporated into your own individual plan. These have been focused on for centuries and are vital elements to building your relationship with the Lord. However, remember that this plan is yours and will have unique elements that help you grow that may not be what others use. So use these as a

---

2. This is not to say that we shouldn't work and make plans in this life. We recognize what our goal is: God. That goal directs all our steps and plans as we seek Him in every aspect of our lives. Therefore, we do not become lazy, but instead work harder to honor Him in this life and the next, just as we desire to express our love and devotion to Him. We seek first His kingdom in every moment of our lives.

3. Matthew 6:2–33.

foundation to develop your own plan, choosing those elements that you know will help you grow the most.

There are three elements we encourage everyone to have when making their own Plan for Spiritual Growth. We didn't come up with these, God did. We are simply highlighting what God has already laid out. We call them "The Greatest Things." In Scripture, we learn what Jesus knew to be the Greatest Commands and the Great Commission. Simply put, "The Greatest Things" are (1) love God, (2) love others, and (3) go and make disciples. Following "The Greatest Things" allows us to create a Plan for Spiritual Growth that honors God in the greatest ways. Let's look at these elements in more detail:

1. **Love God.** To grow in intimacy with God, we must make time to be with Him regularly. Why? Because this is about a relationship with Him. Any relationship requires time with that person to understand them and to grow in our love for them. We must make sure that our relationship with God is the most important relationship we have. To keep our relationship with God thriving and growing, we must spend time with Him to learn about who He is. This will develop that intimacy that we long to have with Him and that He has always longed to have with us. Here are some elements that might aid us in this area of growth.

    a. *Study and meditate on God's Word.* Take time to be in God's Word every day. Find a reading plan that is right for you. It is through God's Word that we get to know Him as He reveals Himself to us through the pages of Scripture. Not only do we learn about God, but also God speaks to us through the words and the stories. Study and meditation is a conversation with God.

    b. *Prayer.* As we have discussed often, prayer is talking to God. It's a conversation. There's no need for big words and long prayers. Just be yourself and talk with Him as you would talk with the person you love the most on this earth. Thank Him every day. Pray for others. Pray for His guidance. Pray for your concerns and those of others. Pray with your eyes closed or open, while sitting or standing, kneeling or lying on your bed, driving in your car, taking a shower, anyplace

> Rejoice always, pray without ceasing, give thanks in all circumstances; for this is the will of God in Christ Jesus for you.
>
> I Thessalonians 5:16–18

> But from there you will seek the Lord your God and you will find him, if you search after him with all your heart and with all your soul.
>
> Deuteronomy 4:29

and anytime. Make prayer a part of every moment of your life. Remember, pray without ceasing.

c. *Practice spiritual disciplines.* We all have a uniqueness that God created in us. Therefore, we will all discover certain spiritual disciplines that will help us connect to God personally in a way that may be different from each other. That's why it is important to discover the spiritual disciplines that help you unite with Christ. For some, the discipline may be journaling, for some it may be worship through music or even art, and for others it may come through practicing hospitality. The point is, find what your spiritual disciplines are by deliberately discovering them. It will take some trial and error, but if you seek God with all your heart and soul, you will find him. The question is, What can you do with your time to draw closer to God?

d. *Join a Bible study or prayer group.* God saw that it was not good for man to be alone. In His great wisdom, God knew that we needed others, and so He created us to live in community. Relationships with others help us grow, but they are also messy. Often, that's why we avoid them. However, we need other disciples to encourage and challenge us in the faith. We must learn from others and pray with them, which gives us an opportunity to connect with God in new ways as we encounter God through the eyes, ears, and hearts of others. While God created us uniquely, He also created all of us in His image. That means that in each person we see a different aspect of God. As we meet with each other, we allow others to see the aspect of God in us, and we see the aspect of God found only in them.

2. **Love others.** Our society has created an illusion that we can encounter God alone and just have a "personal relationship with God" without needing others. However, as we mentioned earlier, God created us to live in community with others. He did not intend for us to walk this journey alone, but instead with the help of other disciples. Remember, our growth in Christ does not happen outside of relationship: relationship with God *and* relationship

with others. Consider those times when you experienced the greatest spiritual growth. Often we associate those moments of growth with the people who helped us through them. With that in mind, here are some elements to aid us in loving others:

a. *Get a spiritual guide or mentor.* The concept of life coaches and counselors are widespread in our society. Why? Because even a secular culture recognizes the need for others to help us grow in different areas of our life. A spiritual guide or mentor is someone you believe will help you grow in your relationship with God. This person is someone who you know will not allow you to settle for the status quo in your relationship with God, but instead will be willing to help you recognize your blind-spots, challenge your thinking, and rebuke you when you are wrong. This person is not the one you would go to tell you what you *want to hear*, but to tell you *what you need to know*. This element is one of the essential elements in true discipleship.

b. *Attend church services and gatherings regularly.* The Bible encourages us to not give up meeting together regularly (Hebrews 10:25). Meeting together is fundamental to our spiritual growth. When we gather together, we learn together and get opportunities to share our lives with other disciples. God speaks to us in this way. So, it is essential to our spiritual growth. God uses other disciples to help us with life's struggles or to give us encouragement when we need it most. God speaks and ministers to us through other disciples. Often, our worship services do not foster that type of relationship. You must not limit yourself to Sunday worship, but instead take the opportunity to join others in Bible classes and other church gatherings that will foster spiritual growth.

c. *Be part of a growth group.* Growth groups are an important context in which we can "carry one another's burdens" and challenge each other toward spiritual growth.

d. *Serve others.* Many opportunities exist to serve people both inside and outside of the church. We typically tell people that if you want to connect with others then go and serve with them.

> And let us consider how to stir up one another to love and good works, not neglecting to meet together, as is the habit of some, but encouraging one another, and all the more as you see the Day drawing near
>
> Hebrews 10:24–25

e. *Become involved in a ministry group.* The church offers many different ministry opportunities. Pray and ask God where He could use you. Ministry groups will help you get connected with other disciples who are seeking to honor God with their lives. Sometimes it takes a little time and can be frustrating. Yet you should commit to a group and seek to discover where God can use you. In doing so, He will connect you with people who will help you grow as a disciple.

f. *Become involved in missions.* Missions are another way not only to serve God, but also to serve others by meeting their physical, spiritual, and emotional needs. It takes us out of our comfort zone and into a world that God wants us to reach. During those opportunities, you are connecting with God, with those serving on the trip with you, and with those whom you are serving. If you feel like your walk with God has grown stale, then go on a mission trip.

3. **Go and make disciples.** The Great Commission calls us to be actively going and making disciples. When we do so, we grow as disciples ourselves. It is a natural by-product of discipling. The more we intentionally go out and disciple others, the more we grow as a disciple. Here are a few elements in accomplishing this task:

    a. *Share your faith with others.* The most obvious way to "go and make disciples" is for you to make a concerted effort to find others you can share your faith with. They can be your neighbors, coworkers, friends, team members, and other people. The question you want to ask yourself is, are you being deliberate about sharing your faith in Christ with them?

    b. *Serve others.* As mentioned, serving others is a great opportunity for sharing your faith with other people.

    c. *Become involved in missions.* As we mentioned earlier, mission trips are a great way for you to go and share your faith and disciple others. For many, they discover that they want to be on the mission field permanently. For others, they discover that the mission field is wherever they find themselves, and they are now better equipped to help those around them become disciples of Christ.

Now that we have briefly described the three elements of spiritual growth, we can move forward in creating our personal Plan for Spiritual Growth. The following pages are intended for you to work through and pray over to make a plan for the coming year. You should do this with others so that you have accountability throughout the year. The intention here is that you are not being reactive in your spiritual growth (engaging things as they come), but proactive (planning for growth). God bless you on your journey!

Plan for Spiritual Growth

Use the following pages to create your Plan for Spiritual Growth. Remember, this process goes on throughout your life. Therefore, you should to do this each year so that you can continue in your growth rather than become complacent and apathetic. There are no "right" or "wrong" answers here. This is your plan. You are not required to do everything each quarter, but do make a strategy as to what you want to do.

Use the help of your accountability partners or discipleship group to help you discover your areas of growth and to hold you to your commitment. Before you begin, spend time in prayer and fasting. Ask God to help you discover the ways in which you can grow closer to Him and help others do so as well. Trust that He will answer you in the affirmative! May God bless you!

Name: _____

Accountability or Discipleship Partner(s): _____
_____
_____
_____

Beginning Date: _____

Current Phase of Spiritual Growth (circle one):

        Spiritual Infancy   Spiritual Childhood   Spiritual Adolescence

                Spiritual Adulthood   Spiritual Maturity

Plan for Spiritual Growth Covenant

I believe that my relationship with God is the most important relationship in my life. Therefore, I give priority to Him in all things. This *Plan for Spiritual Growth* is my covenant between God, my accountability or discipleship partner(s), and me. I ask you, Father, to draw us closer together through these efforts as I open myself up to Your Spirit's transformative work in my life. My desire is that Your Spirit will transform me into the image of Your Son, my Savior, Jesus Christ. May Your will be done in my life!

_____

(My Signature)

_____

(Partner Signature)

_____

(Partner Signature)

First Quarter (the months of _____ to _____)

During this first quarter, I will do the following:

Love God by…

❑ Studying and meditating on God's Word by _____
_____
_____
_____
_____
_____
_____
_____

❑ Praying daily by _____
_____
_____
_____
_____
_____
_____
_____

❑ Practicing Spiritual Disciplines by _____
_____
_____
_____
_____
_____
_____
_____

❑ Being a part of a Bible study or prayer group by _____
_____
_____
_____
_____
_____
_____
_____

❑ Doing the following things to connect with God: _____
_____
_____
_____
_____
_____
_____
_____

Love others by…

❑ Getting a Spiritual Guide or Mentor _____
(name of Guide or Mentor)

❑ Attending church services and gatherings regularly

❑ Being part of a growth group

❑ Serving others by _____
_____
_____
_____
_____
_____
_____

- ❑ Becoming involved in a ministry group (list group or groups): _____
_____
_____
_____
_____
_____
_____

- ❑ Becoming involved in missions by _____
_____
_____
_____
_____
_____
_____

- ❑ Doing the following things to connect with others: _____
_____
_____
_____
_____
_____
_____

Go and make disciples by…

- ❑ Sharing my faith with others by _____
_____
_____
_____
_____
_____

- Serving others by _____
  _____
  _____
  _____
  _____
  _____
  _____
  _____

- Becoming involved in missions by _____
  _____
  _____
  _____
  _____
  _____
  _____
  _____

- Doing the following things to "go and make disciples": _____
  _____
  _____
  _____
  _____
  _____
  _____
  _____

To grow more and more into the image of Christ, I need to repent of and allow the Holy Spirit to change and transform the following areas in my life: _____
_____
_____
_____
_____
_____
_____
_____
_____
_____
_____
_____
_____
_____
_____
_____
_____
_____

Second Quarter (the months of _____ to _____)

During the second quarter, I will do the following:

Love God by…

❏ Studying and meditating on God's Word by _____
_____
_____
_____
_____
_____
_____
_____

❏ Praying daily by _____
_____
_____
_____
_____
_____
_____
_____

❏ Practicing Spiritual Disciplines by _____
_____
_____
_____
_____
_____
_____
_____

❏   Being a part of a Bible study or prayer group by _____
_____
_____
_____
_____
_____
_____

❏   Doing the following things to connect with God: _____
_____
_____
_____
_____
_____
_____
_____

Love others by…

❏   Getting a Spiritual Guide or Mentor _____
(name of Guide or Mentor)

❏   Attending church services and gatherings regularly

❏   Being part of a growth group

❏   Serving others by _____
_____
_____
_____
_____
_____
_____

- ❑ Becoming involved in a ministry group (list group or groups): _____
_____
_____
_____
_____
_____
_____

- ❑ Becoming involved in missions by _____
_____
_____
_____
_____
_____
_____
_____

- ❑ Doing the following things to connect with others: _____
_____
_____
_____
_____
_____
_____

Go and make disciples by…

- ❑ Sharing my faith with others by _____
_____
_____
_____
_____

- Serving others by _____
  _____
  _____
  _____
  _____
  _____
  _____
  _____

- Becoming involved in missions by _____
  _____
  _____
  _____
  _____
  _____
  _____
  _____

- Doing the following things to "go and make disciples": _____
  _____
  _____
  _____
  _____
  _____
  _____
  _____

To grow more and more into the image of Christ, I need to repent of and allow the Holy Spirit to change and transform the following areas in my life: _____
_____
_____
_____
_____
_____
_____
_____
_____
_____
_____
_____
_____
_____
_____
_____
_____

Third Quarter (the months of _____ to _____)

During the third quarter, I will do the following:

Love God by…

- ☐ Studying and meditating on God's Word by _____
  _____
  _____
  _____
  _____
  _____
  _____
  _____

- ☐ Praying daily by _____
  _____
  _____
  _____
  _____
  _____
  _____
  _____

- ☐ Practicing Spiritual Disciplines by _____
  _____
  _____
  _____
  _____
  _____
  _____
  _____

❑ Being a part of a Bible study or prayer group by _____
_____
_____
_____
_____
_____
_____
_____

❑ Doing the following things to connect with God: _____
_____
_____
_____
_____
_____
_____
_____
_____

Love others by…

❑ Getting a Spiritual Guide or Mentor _____

(name of Guide or Mentor)

❑ Attending church services and gatherings regularly.

❑ Being part of a growth group.

❑ Serving others by _____
_____
_____
_____
_____
_____
_____
_____

- ❏ Becoming involved in a ministry group (list group or groups): _____
  _____
  _____
  _____
  _____
  _____
  _____
  _____

- ❏ Becoming involved in missions by _____
  _____
  _____
  _____
  _____
  _____
  _____
  _____

- ❏ Doing the following things to connect with others: _____
  _____
  _____
  _____
  _____
  _____
  _____
  _____

Go and make disciples by…

- ❏ Sharing my faith with others by _____
  _____
  _____
  _____
  _____
  _____

❏ Serving others by _____
_____
_____
_____
_____
_____
_____
_____

❏ Becoming involved in missions by _____
_____
_____
_____
_____
_____
_____
_____

❏ Doing the following things to "go and make disciples": _____
_____
_____
_____
_____
_____
_____

To grow more and more into the image of Christ, I need to repent of and allow the Holy Spirit to change and transform the following areas in my life: _____
_____
_____
_____
_____
_____
_____
_____
_____
_____
_____
_____
_____
_____
_____
_____

Fourth Quarter (the months of _____ to _____)

During this quarter, I will do the following:

Love God by…

❑ Studying and meditating on God's Word by _____
_____
_____
_____
_____
_____
_____

❑ Praying daily by _____
_____
_____
_____
_____
_____
_____

❑ Practicing Spiritual Disciplines by _____
_____
_____
_____
_____
_____
_____

- ❏ Being a part of a Bible study or prayer group by _____
  _____
  _____
  _____
  _____
  _____
  _____
  _____
  _____

- ❏ Doing the following things to connect with God: _____
  _____
  _____
  _____
  _____
  _____
  _____
  _____
  _____

<u>Love others</u> by…

- ❏ Getting a Spiritual Guide or Mentor _____
  (name of Guide or Mentor)

- ❏ Attending church services and gatherings regularly

- ❏ Being part of a growth group

- ❏ Serving others by _____
  _____
  _____
  _____
  _____
  _____
  _____
  _____

❏ Becoming involved in a ministry group (list group or groups): _____
_____
_____
_____
_____
_____
_____
_____

❏ Becoming involved in missions by _____
_____
_____
_____
_____
_____
_____
_____
_____

❏ Doing the following things to connect with others: _____
_____
_____
_____
_____
_____
_____
_____
_____

Go and make disciples by…

❏ Sharing my faith with others by _____
_____
_____
_____
_____
_____

- ❑ Serving others by _____
  _____
  _____
  _____
  _____
  _____
  _____
  _____

- ❑ Becoming involved in missions by _____
  _____
  _____
  _____
  _____
  _____
  _____
  _____

- ❑ Doing the following things to "go and make disciples": _____
  _____
  _____
  _____
  _____
  _____
  _____
  _____

To grow more and more into the image of Christ, I need to repent of and allow the Holy Spirit to change and transform the following areas in my life: _____
_____
_____
_____
_____
_____
_____
_____
_____
_____
_____
_____
_____
_____
_____
_____
_____
_____

Post-Plan Evaluation

Current Phase of Spiritual Growth after this year (circle one):

Spiritual Infancy   Spiritual Childhood   Spiritual Adolescence

Spiritual Adulthood   Spiritual Maturity

What have I learned about myself and my growth as a disciple of Christ? _____
_____
_____
_____
_____
_____
_____
_____
_____
_____
_____
_____
_____
_____
_____
_____
_____

What have I learned about God and my relationship with Him? _____
_____
_____
_____
_____
_____
_____

What are my next steps toward Spiritual Growth?

Chapter 7

The Plan for Discipleship

Discipling Christians involves propelling Christians into the world to risk their lives for the sake of others. The world is our focus at FXCC, and we gauge church success on the hundreds who are leaving our facility (or basecamp) to take on the world with the disciples they are making. Disciple-making takes place multiple times every week in multiple locations by a force of men and women sharing, showing, and teaching the Word of Christ and together serving a world in need of Christ. The indwelling Spirit directs and empowers discipleship and spiritual formation, but we are called to assist each other in becoming like Jesus Christ.

Part of the vision at FXCC is to *deepen biblical understanding that increases spiritual maturity* by studying, teaching, and discipling others through God's Word. Spiritual maturity, passion, and commitment to Christ are marked by an ever-increasing desire to follow Christ wherever He leads and is developed through the identification and use of gifts provided by the Holy Spirit to serve others (1 Peter 2:1–3; 1 Corinthians 3:1–4; Ephesians 4:11–16; Hebrews 5:12; Romans 12:3–7).

We want to be intentional with that desire by providing a plan that leads us all toward spiritual maturity. The following is our coordinated and prayerfully, Spirit-led effort toward developing the Plan for Discipleship and Spiritual Formation at FXCC to ensure that church efforts (through various ministries) contribute in some way to our mission for discipleship: making devoted followers of Jesus Christ who passionately lead others to Him.

The Plan for Discipleship at FXCC

The following is our plan for discipleship at FXCC, as well as specific information on each item. Many people in the world today claim to believe or follow Jesus. However, "believing in" or "following Jesus" is not always the same thing as being a disciple of Jesus. In fact, following Jesus by today's terms can be equated with following someone on Twitter. Just because you follow someone, doesn't mean you are trying to become like him or her. We believe that in order to truly be a disciple of Christ, we must be intentional with the "how."

Therefore, one of our priorities and goals here at FXCC is to be intentional with our discipleship efforts and toward helping each member grow toward Christlikeness. Not only is our plan intentional, but it is also a daily plan. As Jesus told His disciples, "If anyone would come after me, let him deny himself and take up his cross *daily* and follow me."[4] We encourage our family members to follow Jesus daily by using what we call "The Seven E Words" as a guide.

The Seven E Words

In Scripture, the number seven represents the thought of completeness or perfection. We believe that if members consistently practice the Seven E Words, then they will progressively grow more and more in Christlikeness. As with any well-laid plan, there are *daily*, *weekly*, and *monthly* goals. So to grow as a disciple of Christ, we encourage each family member to do the following.

---

4. Luke 9:23 (emphasis added).

⤢ EXPAND...*your knowledge (or knowing) of God through daily Bible reading.*

Daily

Not on Bread Alone Menu (Bible Reading Plan)

Our Not on Bread Alone (NOBA) Menu (see Appendix B) is our yearly Bible reading plan. Our desire is for every member to read through God's Word each year. We believe that intentionally being in God's Word is a vital part of growing as a disciple of Christ. We call this a menu because we believe that the intake of God's Word is as important (if not more important) than the intake of physical food. In the same way that a well-balanced diet of physical food can cause growth, so also a full and well-balanced diet of God's Word can cause exponential spiritual growth. However, an unbalanced diet of God's Word can cause stagnancy and ultimately spiritual death if we go too long without it. As Jesus quoted from Deuteronomy 8:3, "It is written, 'Man shall not live by bread alone, but by every word that comes from the mouth of God.'" Jesus knew that the Word is God's nourishment for His children.

Deuteronomy 30:14 says, "No, the word is very near you; it is in your mouth and in your heart so you may obey it." God's Word is the spiritual food we eat to grow and become more like Christ. With this understanding of the Word of God, we must see Scripture as more than *informational*; it also needs to be more *formational*. We must begin to see God's Word with different eyes. Not as words on a page, but words in our hearts. As the Word dwells in us, it begins to shape us from the inside out. But if it does not take up residence in our hearts, then it is simply information in our heads that may only be occasionally accessed and used. When the Word is not in our mouths and in our hearts, THE WORD (Jesus) is not in our mouths and in our hearts. When we are biblically illiterate, we are God/Jesus/Spirit illiterate. We don't worship the Word; we worship THE WORD. However, we come to know THE WORD through the Word. But we must caution you here: Consuming these menu items will only increase your appetite for growth in regards to your heart, soul, mind, and strength (Deuteronomy 6:4–5). So beware!

We encourage each of our members to have a steady intake of God's Word. This particular reading plan was designed by The Navigators[5] and is called the *Discipleship Journal Reading Plan.* The plan takes you to four separate places in Scripture each day to help you better understand the unity of God's Word amid four differing viewpoints. It is also designed to help you not fall too far behind by scheduling 25 days of reading each month. This leaves you with five to six "free days" to either catch up or read further on your own.

This reading plan also aligns well with our **six-year curriculum scope and sequence** (see Appendix C). That way, you will be reading in the areas of Scripture that will be taught in Bible classes from children, youth, and adult studies. Our hope is to approach our formation as disciples holistically so that we may have common conversations about God's Word and what it is revealing to us at any given time of the year with any given group or individual in the church family. We hope that the NOBA Menu provides guidance for the study of Scripture from individual (personal Bible study and devotion), to group (Bible classes, study groups, discipleship groups), to congregational (sermons, growth groups) perspectives. Our goal is to provide a common place to come together in our spiritual growth and nurturance.

> Daily

EXTEND...*your knowledge and understanding of God through a committed time of prayer each day.*

We believe that committed times of prayer are vital to our spiritual formation and discipleship. Therefore, we ask each of our members to engage in a devoted time of prayer each day. Our hope is that this time of prayer will expand over time, but at first we encourage each member to commit to spending time with God in prayer at least once a day. In asking for this commitment, we recognize that it is important to understand what prayer really is:

- **Relationship.** Relating to God one-on-one for intimacy
- **Reliance.** Relying on God for everything

---

5. For more information, go to www.navigators.org and click on tools to find this Bible reading plan.

- **Recognition.** Recognizing God's presence and sovereignty in your life
- **Remembrance.** Remembering who God is, what He does, and what He wants
- **Rest.** Resting in Him as the one who is in control and looking out for your best interest

EXPRESS…*your new knowledge of God and His Word through regular memorization of Scripture.*

Weekly

Why is Scripture memorization one of the Seven E Words? Simply put, there is no greater way to get to know God and His ways than through His Word. Dallas Willard once said,

> Bible memorization is absolutely fundamental to spiritual formation. If I had to choose between all the disciplines of the spiritual life, I would choose Bible memorization, because it is a fundamental way of filling our minds with what it needs. This book of the law shall not depart out of your mouth. That's where you need it! How does it get in your mouth? Memorization.[6]

We believe that memorization is vital to discipleship because God's Word planted in our hearts

- Helps us come to know who God is and what He asks of us
- Provides us with ways to overcome sin
- Helps us overcome Satan
- Helps us communicate God's gospel message to those who do not believe
- Is His way of communicating to us. As prayer is our way to talk with God. Study is His way of talking to us.

For those reasons, we ask individuals to memorize some portion of Scripture each week to meditate on the things of God and to place those things on their hearts for ready recollection.

---

6. Dallas Willard, "Spiritual Formation in Christ for the Whole Life and Whole Person," *VOCATIO* 12, no. 2 (Spring 2001), p. 7.

Weekly

🔍 **EXPLORE**...*the deeper meanings of God's Word through consistent group Bible studies for accountability and to understand how Scripture affects your daily walk and your place in God's story.*

BIBLE CLASSES (six-year Coordinated Curriculum Plan)

We believe that Bible study in the midst of other believers is an important part of our spiritual formation and discipleship. Therefore, we ask that all our members regularly take part in a Sunday morning Bible class in order to explore God's Word with other brothers and sisters in Christ so that mutual growth can take place. We have three goals with each of our Bible classes taught at FXCC:

1. **Transformation.** Through the study of God's Word with other fellow disciples, our desire is that hearts will be spiritually transformed and lives changed. We do not study to simply gain information. Instead, we study for transformation so that God may change us from the inside out. We hope that Bible class participants, through the study of Scripture, are drawn into an intimate relationship with Jesus Christ.
2. **Fellowship.** Transformation often happens in the midst of community. In that community one finds encouragement, motivation, accountability, and often loving correction. One of the goals we have with our Bible classes is to take individuals from various backgrounds, ages, and personalities and to help create an environment where authentic relationships can be formed for the purpose of spiritual formation and discipleship.
3. **Multiplication.** As members grow spiritually through our Bible studies, we hope that it will spur them on to go and make disciples of others and to lead Bible studies of their own.

With those goals in mind, our Sunday morning Bible studies have a two-fold purpose:

1. We hope and pray that all class participants will gain a better knowledge and understanding of the biblical books or topics being studied so that they may grow spiritually by knowing more about God and His overall plan of redemption (His will and purpose for our lives).

2. We hope and pray that this knowledge and understanding will lead our family members to demonstrate their wisdom of God's Word by sharing it with those around them (that is, at school, at work). Having knowledge about a topic of study does not mean an internal change has been made that brings about action.
    a. The first step *is* to gain the knowledge (a matter of the **head**).
    b. But then the longest journey begins, and it is only 12 inches. That 12-inch journey is going deeper with the knowledge to the point that you understand it (a matter of moving it from the **head** to the **heart**).
    c. The final step is to move from understanding to wisdom. This step is demonstrated through people's actions. When people take what they know and understand and put it into practice, they demonstrate Godly wisdom (moving from the **heart** to the **hands** [Matthew 7:24–27]).

So in our Bible classes, we hope to provide material that will provide knowledge (**head**), then ask questions that will bring us understanding (**heart**), and then motivate participants to go and live the Word in the world and to demonstrate Godly wisdom (**hands**).

HEAD → HEART → HANDS

We hope that through our Bible studies our class participants not only will hear, know, and understand the Word, but will also be driven to become the "Living Word" to the world around them. We constantly ask our Bible class teachers and facilitators to go beyond the lessons or curriculum to demonstrate how what they teach can and should be lived daily. We are all the 67th book of Scripture as we engage the world with the Word of God, and we pray our Bible classes better equip us for that engagement.

GROWTH GROUPS

FXCC is committed to providing multiple opportunities for our people to connect and grow in their relationship with Christ and with others. Therefore, we ask all our members (as a part of their development as a disciple of Christ) to participate in a growth group.

What is a growth group? It's pretty simple. A growth group is a small group of people (usually no more than 15 to 20 adults) who gather in homes throughout the metro area. Some meet on Sundays and others meet throughout the week. Some groups meet in the evening while others meet earlier in the day. Some share a meal together and others do not. Some have children present all or part of the time and others have no children.

Our growth groups offer fellowship, prayer, study in God's Word, service projects, outreach opportunities, and mutual support and encouragement in our faith journeys. No matter what design our growth groups take, they *all* provide opportunities for each participant to *grow*.

The purpose for our growth groups is to provide growth in (1) individual spiritual maturity, (2) relationships and connections with the Body of Christ, and (3) bringing others to Christ and into the Body of Christ. We want to help our members and guests experience transformed lives. Whether one is just now becoming interested in God or has walked with him for many years, a growth group will be a powerful resource in one's quest to be transformed into the image of Christ.

Do you want to find out who is in a growth group and what they are doing? Do you want to visit with them and see if the group would be a good fit? Contact the church office at church.office@fxcc.org or 703-631-2100. We will do everything we can to help you find a growth group that is right for you.

DISCIPLESHIP GROUPS

True discipleship is mutual and relational in nature. Why? Because relationships are the conduit of God's love. Therefore, we want to help our members focus on becoming more like Christ by building relationships with others, meeting regularly with them, and holding each other accountable as brothers and sisters in Christ. To accomplish this, we want to help our members to

- Identify two to three individuals (for groups of no more than 4 individuals) whom they can meet with regularly during the coming year (1-year commitment) to grow as a disciple of Christ.

- Have a mentor who works to develop personal relationships with the individuals so that out of a relationship of love and trust one might begin to grow toward spiritual maturity.
- Spend time together going through the Discipleship Curriculum "Covered in Dust" together.[7]
- Work together to develop a personal growth plan based on the results of the assessments and the desired level of spiritual maturity the disciple would like to accomplish during the year with the discipleship group.

EXPERIENCE...*God by regularly practicing spiritual disciplines that are designed to give space to God in your life.*

Weekly

Spiritual disciplines are designed to open up space in our lives that is needed for God to meet with us, transform us, and prepare us for His work. Spiritual disciplines are not received the same by every person. One may impact one individual and not another. Please remember that they are a means and not the end. Trying new practices regularly will help us to discover new ways to see and connect with God. It is a good practice to try new ones often to see which one the Spirit may be speaking to you through. In the end, the goal is to grow more intimate with God and to hear His voice. We want our members to get spiritual exercise with at least one spiritual disciple each week to grow closer with God.

EQUIP...*yourself for the work of ministry and to build up the body of Christ by consistent participation in the body of Christ at FXCC (Sunday morning worship, Wednesday evenings, retreats, conferences).*

Weekly/Monthly

WORSHIP

We believe that worship is a part of what forms adults and children into or away from a Christ-centered faith. It affects the way we live

---

7. See Appendix D for more details concerning our "Covered in Dust" curriculum.

every day. Therefore, choosing one thing over another is more than a matter of taste and preference in worship! It is a responsibility and an opportunity for discipleship and spiritual formation.

The Latin phrase *lex orandi, lex credendi, lex vivendi* essentially means "how we pray influences what we believe and how we live our lives." By this we understand that all aspects of worship influence discipleship and spiritual formation, both for individuals and for those who have gathered for worship. As we have already noted, spiritual formation can be anything, Christ-centered or not, that forms us from the inside out. Everyone is being formed spiritually, whether for good or evil. What we read, watch, sing, and listen to contributes to the formation of our inner self (soul, spirit).

The world understands that all too well as advertisers use the concept as a way to shape thought. They don't call it spiritual formation, but they understand that if you change someone's thoughts, then you change their actions. Advertisers spend billions of dollars each year to have us believe that their product will somehow make us better. Spiritual formation that happens through television, movies, magazines, and other media is hours longer than the spiritual formation and discipleship that happens through worship each week.

While much of this formation happens unconsciously, we must be conscious of and intentional with what is happening every Sunday in worship. Choosing songs, Scriptures, sermon topics or series, and communion thoughts will contribute to or hinder people's ability to pray, believe, and ultimately live each day well as a disciple of Christ.

With that in mind, our worship is fairly simple and designed to keep the focus on God, not ourselves. As you can imagine, every Sunday worship assembly isn't exactly the same, but there are some common ingredients we mix in every week to help us come before the throne of God; to worship Him with all our heart, soul, mind, and strength; and to be formed into the image of Jesus Christ.

WEDNESDAY EVENINGS

On Wednesday evenings, we offer a time of food, fellowship, and Bible study for all ages. We desire to offer a mid-week time for reflection on the week past and the week ahead, and how we might honor God in our lives. The studies will take us deeper into our growing relationships with God and each other in the midst of the busyness of life. We also want our Wednesday evenings to provide a weekly opportunity for our discipleship groups to meet if they need a time already set aside. We ask members to come and expect to meet up with God (either through the Bible study provided or discipleship groups), and we'll do our best to provide opportunities to learn and grow each week.

RETREATS, SEMINARS, AND CONFERENCES

At FXCC, we offer periodic retreats, seminars, and conferences designed specifically to help people grow in their faith and relationship with Christ. Some of them are offered at FXCC and some are away at other locations and organized by different groups and organizations. We encourage members to take part in these gatherings regularly for growth, fellowship, and connecting with other disciples who are ever seeking to become more like Christ.

🌐 ENGAGE...*the world around you through a committed and consistent response to Him (that is, acts of service, outreach, evangelism).*

Monthly

Part of the Great Commission calls us to "go" and "make." We are called as disciples of Christ to go out into the world so that we can be God's light to all people. Jesus shared these words on the sermon on the mount:

> You are the light of the world. A city set on a hill cannot be hidden. Nor do people light a lamp and put it under a basket, but on a stand, and it gives light to all in the house. In the same way, let your light shine before others, so that they may see your good works and give glory to your Father who is in heaven.[8]

God calls us to be His light to the world. By that, we understand Him to say that a disciple of Christ is God's servant who actively engages the world by helping others in practical ways. Like Christ, we did not become His disciples to be served, but to serve others. We understand

---

8. Matthew 5:14–16.

that to serve is to sacrifice and to sacrifice is to give up what may be best for ourselves for the good of others and for the glory of God.

So, we ask our members to share in serving God and His people in some way *at least once a month* as a part of our plan for discipleship. We hope that each person works each day to be a living sacrifice to God. However, we ask that everyone start with at least one act of service each month with hopes that it will grow month after month and week after week.

Acts of service (or the go and make in the Great Commission) come in many different forms. People only need to open their eyes and see the needs of those around them. God will always present opportunities to engage the world around you through meeting the needs of others, whether those needs are physical or spiritual. (Of course, we all recognize that in meeting physical needs we often meet spiritual needs.) There are many opportunities to serve people both inside and outside of the church. We typically tell people that if you want to connect with others, then go and serve with them.

Part of our acts of serving God includes going and being a witness for God. We have the unique privilege of sharing His message of salvation. A disciple intentionally shares his or her faith in Jesus regularly with those who do not know the Lord. It is an honor to share the love and grace of God (given through Christ) that has been freely given to us so that others may know and share in it with us. There are three specific ways we encourage everyone to live out this goal of engaging the world through service to God:

1. **Share your faith with others**. The most obvious way to go and make is for you to make a concerted effort to find others you can share your faith with. They can be your neighbors, coworkers, friends, team members, or other people. The point is that you are being deliberate about sharing your faith in Christ with them.
2. **Serve others**. As mentioned, serving others by meeting their physical needs is a great opportunity for you to share your faith with them. This can be in the form of giving food to the hungry, providing shelter for the homeless, giving clothes to those without, providing funds for the poor, and many other ways. The options are endless, but those willing to serve are often few. Seek to discover some way each month to serve others rather than yourself.

3. **Becoming involved in missions.** Missions are another way to serve not only God, but also others by meeting their physical, spiritual, and emotional needs. It takes us out of our comfort zone and into a world that God wants us to reach. During those opportunities, you are connecting with God, with those serving with you on the trip, and with those whom you are serving. If you feel like your walk with God has grown stale, then go on a mission trip. Some discover on a mission trip that they want to be in the mission field permanently. For others, they discover that the mission field is wherever they find themselves, and they are now better equipped to help those around them become disciples of Christ.

Jesus said, "It is more blessed to give than receive."[9] We believe those words with all our hearts. Although some people are truly gifted by the Holy Spirit in this area, we firmly believe that the Bible teaches us that all disciples are to engage the world through good works. We ask all our members to join us in these efforts as true disciples of Jesus Christ.

The Plan in Action

There you have it! The Plan for Discipleship at FXCC. In the preceding pages, we hope that we have outlined for you what we believe God is asking of us as His disciples. As you may have noted, much of what we said so far in this chapter has focused more on what you can do as an individual (although most of what we have encouraged is meant to be shared in community rather than isolation). However, we also want to share with you how this emphasis on discipleship and spiritual formation will be seen throughout the overall ministry of Fairfax Church of Christ.

Each ministry area (that is, discipleship, outreach, family life, and coordination) has worked with its ministries and ministry leads to focus on *making devoted followers of Jesus Christ who passionately lead others to Him*. We want everything we do to be done with this purpose and mission in mind. This mission is demonstrated in greater detail in our

---

9. Acts 20:35.

Vision, Mission, and Values for FXCC (see Appendix E). We want everything we do to be seen through this lens.

Each ministry lead at FXCC has spent time going through this plan and looking deeper into what is being done in their ministry and why. Each ministry has asked the following question regarding what they do, "How does this _____ (fill in the blank) help successfully execute making devoted followers of Jesus Christ who passionately lead others to Him?"

After answering this question for each ministry activity, event, study, series, etc., the ministry leads then looked at how each budget dollar spent is going toward the mission and purpose. With painstaking work, each ministry was assessed at FXCC and led toward this overarching mission of God. The leadership team (elders, staff members, MCT) has dedicated its members to carry out this mission both individually and through leadership in every avenue of FXCC's focus and ministry.

We recognized that to truly carry out this purpose and mission we have to be "all in." All in means our leaders must be practicing what we are teaching and preaching. Going all in means recognizing that we must not do some things we are currently doing to allow time for intentional discipleship. The leadership at FXCC firmly believes this is God's call, His mission, and His purpose for us both individually and as a family. Therefore, we are working toward this mission every day.

We believe that an emphasis in what it means to be a disciple of Christ at FXCC and providing this plan of implementation and direction for discipleship will help us be more purposed, coordinated, communicated, and assessed in every aspect of ministry at FXCC. This will become the filter through which we dream, plan, implement, and assess all that we do.

We recognize that we will have times in which we will fall short of this goal. We will make mistakes and sometimes take wrong paths. However, we will not allow shortcomings to halt God's progress in us, as weak as we are. For we believe that God's power is made perfect through our weakness. For when we are weak, HE makes us strong.[10]

Therefore, we move forward with this mission in mind. We do so unapologetically and with great zeal to no longer make excuses for

---

10. See 2 Corinthians 12:1–10.

why we have not carried out God's Greatest Things (loving God, loving others, going and making disciples). Instead, we are full of resolve to make every effort to become and be the disciples that Jesus has called us to be. We ask that every member of Fairfax Church of Christ join in these efforts together as a family so that we (both individually and collectively) can bring glory and honor to God and can allow His light to shine through us in this dark world. May all we do be pleasing to Him, our God and our King! Through God we GO.

Appendix A

Resources for Discipleship and Spiritual Formation

Whether you are looking for the right topic for your personal spiritual growth, for the growth of your discipleship group, or for someone who you are intentionally discipling, this appendix can help you find a resource that most appropriately matches your needs. We have categorized the resources in a way that we hope you will find easy to understand and locate the particular study you are looking for. The following pages are a culmination of years of study and research in the area of Discipleship and Spiritual Formation.

Please note: We do not necessarily espouse any opinions, views, and interpretations of Scripture or Theology found within these texts. Individuals should read all these texts through the lens of God's Word and decide whether the authors are in line with what the Bible teaches. We have simply listed the texts as resources for further study and growth. Please use godly discernment when reading extra-biblical texts.

Discipleship

Andrews, Alan, ed. *The Kingdom Life: A Practical Theology of Discipleship and Spiritual Formation.* Colorado Springs, CO: NavPress, 2010.

Bonhoeffer, Dietrich. *Discipleship.* Minneapolis, MN: Fortress Press, 2001.

Campbell, Regi, and Richard Chancy. *Mentor Like Jesus.* Nashville, TN: B&H Publishing Group, 2009.

Chan, Francis, and Mark Beuving. *Multiply: Disciples Making Disciples.* First edition. Colorado Springs, CO: David C Cook, 2012.

Gallaty, Robby. *Growing Up: How to Be a Disciple Who Makes Disciples.* Nashville, TN: B&H Publishing Group, 2013.

Gallaty, Robby F., and Ed Stetzer. *Rediscovering Discipleship: Making Jesus' Final Words Our First Work.* Grand Rapids, MI: Zondervan, 2015.

Geiger, Eric, Michael Kelley, and Philip Nation. *Transformational Discipleship: How People Really Grow.* Nashville, TN: B&H Publishing Group, 2012.

Hull, Bill. *The Complete Book of Discipleship: On Being and Making Followers of Christ.* Colorado Springs, CO: NavPress, 2006.

McCallum, Dennis, and Jessica Lowery. *Organic Disciplemaking: Mentoring Others Into Spiritual Maturity and Leadership.* Houston: TOUCH Publications, 2006.

Ogden, Greg. *Transforming Discipleship: Making Disciples a Few at a Time.* Downers Grove, IL: InterVarsity Press, 2003.

———. *Discipleship Essentials: A Guide to Building Your Life in Christ.* Expanded ed. Downers Grove, IL: IVP Connect, 2007.

Putman, Jim. *Real-Life Discipleship: Building Churches That Make Disciples.* Colorado Springs, CO: NavPress, 2010.

———. *DiscipleShift: Five Steps That Help Your Church to Make Disciples Who Make Disciples.* Exponential Series. Grand Rapids, MI: Zondervan, 2013.

Putman, Jim, Bill Krause, Avery Willis, and Brandon Guindon. *Real-Life Discipleship Training Manual: Equipping Disciples Who Make Disciples.* Teacher's Guide edition. Colorado Springs, CO: NavPress, 2010.

Tippens, Darryl. *Pilgrim Heart: The Way of Jesus in Everyday Life.* Abilene, TX: Leafwood Publishers, 2006.

Waggoner, Brad J. *The Shape of Faith to Come: Spiritual Formation and the Future of Discipleship.* Nashville, TN: B&H Publishing Group, 2008.

Wilkins, Michael J. *Following the Master: Discipleship in the Steps of Jesus.* Grand Rapids, MI: Zondervan, 1992.

Yoder, John Howard, John C. Nugent, Andy Alexis-Baker, and Branson L. Parler. *Radical Christian Discipleship.* Harrisonburg, VA: Herald Press, 2012.

History of Spirituality and Spiritual Classics

Anonymous. *The Cloud of Unknowing.* San Francisco: Harper, 2004.

Augustine. *Confessions.* Translated and introduction by R.S. Pine-Coffin. London: Penguin Books, 1961.

Benedict, Anthony C. Meisel, and M. L. Del Mastro. *The Rule of St. Benedict.* Garden City, NY: Image Books, 1975.

Bernard of Clairvaux. *The Love of God.* Edited by James M. Houston. Portland, OR: Multnomah Press, 1983.

Berthold, George C., trans. *Maximus Confessor: Selected Writings.* Notes by George C. Berthold. Mahwah, NJ: Paulist Press, 1985.

Brother Lawrence. *The Practice of the Presence of God.* New Kensington, PA: Whitaker House, 1982.

Bushnell, Horace. *Christian Nurture.* New Haven, CT: Yale, 1861.

Calvin, John. *The Institutes of the Christian Religion.* Edited by John T. McNeill and translated by Ford Lewis Battles. Philadelphia: Westminster Press, 1960.

Calvin, John. *John Calvin: Writings on Pastoral Piety.* Edited by Elsie Anne McKee. Mahwah, NJ: Paulist Press, 2001.

Caussade, Jean Pierre de. *The Sacrament of the Present Moment.* 1st Harper & Row paperback edition. San Francisco: Harper & Row, 1982.

Caussade, Jean Pierre de. *Abandonment to Divine Providence: With Letters of Father De Caussade on the Practice of Self-Abandonment.* San Francisco, CA: Ignatius Press, 2011.

Cornick, David. *Letting God Be God: The Reformed Tradition*. Maryknoll, NY: Orbis Books, 2008.

Cox, Harvey. *Fire from Heaven: The Rise of Pentecostal Spirituality and the Reshaping of Religion in the Twenty-First Century*. Reading, MA: Addison-Wesley Publishing, 1995.

Dupre, Louis and James A. Wiseman, eds. *Light from Light: An Anthology of Christian Mysticism*. Second edition. Mahwah, NJ: Paulist Press, 2001.

Dyck, Cornelius J., ed. *Spiritual Life in Anabaptism: Classic Devotional Resources*. Scottdale, PA: Herald Press, 1995.

Edwards, Jonathan. *Religious Affections: A Christian's Character Before God*. Edited by James M. Houston. Minneapolis: Bethany House Publishers, 1996.

Flinders, Carol. *Enduring Grace: Living Portraits of Seven Women Mystics*. San Francisco, CA: HarperSanFrancisco, 1993.

Foster, Richard J. *Streams of Living Water: Celebrating the Great Traditions of Christian Faith*. First edition. San Francisco: HarperSanFrancisco, 1998.

Foster, Richard J., and James Bryan Smith, eds. *Devotional Classics: Selected Readings for Individuals and Groups*. Revised and expanded. San Francisco: HarperSanFrancisco, 2005.

Francis of Assisi, and Bonaventure. *The Little Flowers of St. Francis; The Mirror of Perfection; St. Bonaventure's Life of St. Francis*. London: Dent, 1976.

French, R.M., trans. *The Way of a Pilgrim and The Pilgrim Continues His Way*. New York: Seabury, 1965.

Gordon, James M. *Evangelical Spirituality: From the Wesleys to John Stott*. London: SPCK, 1991.

Guyon, Jeanne. *Experiencing the Depths of Jesus Christ*. Auburn, MA: Christian Books Publishing House, 1975.

Harmless, William. *Desert Christians: An Introduction to the Literature of Early Monasticism*. Oxford and New York: Oxford University Press, 2004.

———. *Mystics*. New York: Oxford University Press, 2008.

Holt, Bradley P. *Thirsty for God: A Brief History of Christian Spirituality*. Second edition. Minneapolis: Fortress Press, 2005.

Ignatius, and George E. Ganss. *Ignatius of Loyola: The Spiritual Exercises and Selected Works*. New York: Paulist Press, 1991.

Ilibagiza, Immaculee. *Left to Tell: Discovering God Amidst the Rwandan Holocaust*. New York: Hay House, 2007.

John of the Cross. *The Collected Works of St. John of the Cross*. Translated by Kieran Kavanaugh and Otilio Rodriguez. Washington, DC: ICS, 1991.

———. *Dark Night of the Soul*. New York: Image Books/Doubleday, 2005.

Keller, David G. R. *Oasis of Wisdom: The Worlds of the Desert Fathers and Mothers*. Collegeville, MN: Liturgical Press, 2005.

Kelly, Thomas R. *A Testament of Devotion*. San Francisco: HarperSanFrancisco, 1996.

Kempis, Thomas à. *The Imitation of Christ: How Jesus Wants Us to Live*. First edition. Translated by William Griffin. San Francisco: HarperSanFrancisco, 2000.

Kierkegaard, Søren. *Purity of Heart Is to Will One Thing: Spiritual Preparation for the Office of Confession*. Translated by Douglas V. Steere. New York: Harper, 1956.

Kolb, Robert, and Timothy J. Wengert, ed. *The Book of Concord: The Confessions of the Evangelical Lutheran Church*. Minneapolis: Fortress Press, 2000.

Lane, Belden. *Solace of Fierce Landscapes: Exploring Desert and Mountain Spirituality*. New York: Oxford University Press, 1998.

Land, Steven J. *Pentecostal Spirituality: A Passion for the Kingdom*. Sheffield, England: Sheffield Academic Press, 1994.

Lane, Tony. *A Concise History of Christian Thought*. Revised edition. Grand Rapids, MI: Baker Academic, 2006.

Magill, Frank N., and Ian P. McGreal. *Christian Spirituality: The Essential Guide to the Most Influential Writings of the Christian Tradition*. New York: Harper Row, 1988.

McGinn, Bernard. *The Doctors of the Church: Thirty-Three Men and Women Who Shaped Christianity*. New York: Crossroad, 1999.

McGinn, Bernard, ed. *The Essential Writings of Christian Mysticism*. New York: Modern Library Classics/Random House, 2006.

McGuckin, John Anthony. *Standing in God's Holy Fire: The Byzantine Tradition*. Maryknoll, NY: Orbis Books, 2001.

Morden, Peter J. *'Communion with Christ and His People': The Spirituality of C. H. Spurgeon*. Center for Baptist History and Heritage Studies, Volume 5. Oxford: Regent Park College, 2010.

Müller, George. *The Autobiography of George Müller*. New Kensington, PA: Whitaker House, 1985.

Murray, Andrew. *With Christ in the School of Prayer*. Springdale, PA: Whitaker House, 1981.

———. *Absolute Surrender: And Other Addresses*. Hall of Faith Classics 4. New York, NY: G.I.L. Publications, 2015.

Mursell, Gordon. *English Spirituality: From Earliest Times to 1700*. Louisville, KY: Westminster John Knox Press, 2001.

———. *English Spirituality: From 1700 to the Present*. Louisville, KY: Westminster John Knox Press, 2001.

———, ed. *The Story of Christian Spirituality: Two Thousand Years, from East to West*. Minneapolis: Fortress Press, 2001.

Nouwen, Henri J. M. *With Open Hands*. Notre Dame, IN: Ave Maria Press, 1972.

———. *The Genesee Diary*. Garden City, NY: Image Books, 1976.

———. *Making All Things New: An Invitation to the Spiritual Life*. First edition. San Francisco: Harper & Row, 1981.

———. *The Way of the Heart: Desert Spirituality and Contemporary Ministry*. New York: Seabury, 1981.

———. *Reaching Out: The Three Movements of the Spiritual Life*. Garden City, NY: Image Books, 1986.

———. *The Beauty of the Lord: Praying with Icons*. Notre Dame, IN: Ave Maria Press, 1987.

———. *In the Name of Jesus: Reflections on Christian Leadership*. New York: Crossroad, 1989.

———. *Life of the Beloved: Spiritual Living in a Secular World*. New York: Crossroad, 1992.

———. *Ministry and Spirituality*. Revised and compiled edition. New York: Continuum, 1996.

———. *Out of Solitude: Three Meditations on the Christian Life*. First revised edition. Notre Dame, IN: Ave Maria Press, 2004.

Paris, Peter J. *The Spirituality of African Peoples: The Search for a Common Moral Discourse*. Minneapolis: Fortress Press, 1995.

Randall, Ian. *What a Friend We Have in Jesus: The Evangelical Tradition*. London: Darton, Longman, and Todd, 2005.

Sales, Francis de. *Introduction to the Devout Life*. New York: Vintage Books, 2002.

Schmidt, Richard H. *God Seekers: Twenty Centuries of Christian Spiritualties*. Grand Rapids, MI: Eerdmans, 2008.

Schwanda, Tom. "'Hearts Sweetly Refreshed': Puritan Spiritual Practices Then and Now." *Journal of Spiritual Formation and Soul Care* 3, no. 1 (Spring 2010): 21–41.

Selderhuis, Herman. *John Calvin: A Pilgrim's Life*. Downers Grove, IL: InterVarsity Press, 2009.

Senn, Frank C. *Protestant Spiritual Traditions*. Mahwah, NJ: Paulist, 1986.

Sheldrake, Philip. *A Brief History of Spirituality*. Oxford and Malden, MA: Blackwell Publishing, 2007.

Sheldrake, Philip F. *Explorations in Spirituality: History, Theology, and Social Practice*. Mahwah, NJ: Paulist Press, 2010.

Sittser, Gerald L. *Water from a Deep Well: Christian Spirituality from Early Martyrs to Modern Missionaries*. Downers Grove, IL: InterVarsity Press, 2007.

Teresa of Avila. *The Interior Castle*. The Classics of Western Spirituality. New York: Paulist Press, 1979.

———. *The Way of Perfection*. Translated by E. Allison Peers. Garden City, NY: Image Books, 1991.

———. *A Life of Prayer*. Edited by Clayton Burg and James M. Houston. Colorado Springs, CO: David C. Cook Publishers, 2005.

Tozer, A.W. *The Knowledge of the Holy*. San Francisco: HarperSanFrancisco, 1961.

———. *The Pursuit of Man: The Divine Conquest of the Human Heart*. Mass market edition. A Spiritual Classic. Camp Hill, PA: Christian Publications, 1978.

———. *Keys to the Deeper Life*. Revised and expanded. Clarion Classics. Grand Rapids, MI: Zondervan, 1988.

———. *The Pursuit of God*. Camp Hill, PA: Christian Publications, 1993.

Underhill, Evelyn. *The Spiritual Life*. Harrisburg, PA: Morehouse Publishing, 1991.

———. *Evelyn Underhill: Essential Writings*. Modern Spiritual Masters Series. Maryknoll, NY: Orbis Books, 2003.

Waddel, Helen. *The Desert Fathers*. New York: Vintage Books, 1998.

Tyson, John R. *Invitation to Christian Spirituality: An Ecumenical Anthology*. New York: Oxford University Press, 1999.

Woods, Richard J. *Christian Spirituality: God's Presence Through the Ages*. Expanded edition. Maryknoll, NY: Orbis Books, 2006.

Prayer

Baillie, John. *A Diary of Private Prayer*. New York: Scribner, 1938.

Bennett, Arthur, ed. *The Valley of Vision: A Collection of Puritan Prayers & Devotions*. Edinburgh: The Banner of Truth Trust, 1975.

Bloom, Anthony. *Courage to Pray*. New York: Paulist Press, 1973.

———. *Beginning to Pray*. Mahwah, NJ: Paulist Press, 1975.

Bounds, Edward M. *Power through Prayer*. New edition. New Kensington, PA: Whitaker House, 2005.

Bourgeault, Cynthia. *Centering Prayer and Inner Awakening*. Lanham, MD: Cowley Publishers, 2004.

Casey, Michael. *Toward God: The Ancient Wisdom of Western Prayer*. Liguori, MO: Triumph Books, 1996.

DeSilva, David. *Sacramental Life: Spiritual Formation Through the Book of Common Prayer*. Downers Grove, IL: InterVarsity Press, 2008.

Fosdick, Harry Emerson. *The Meaning of Prayer*. Nashville, TN: Abingdon Press, 1962.

Foster, Richard J. *Prayer: Finding the Heart's True Home*. First edition. San Francisco: HarperSanFrancisco, 1992.

Guyon, Jeanne. *Experiencing God Through Prayer*. Updated edition. New Kensington, PA: Whitaker House, 2004.

Hallesby, Ole. *Prayer*. Translated by Clarence J. Carlsen. Minneapolis: Augsburg, 1959.

Job, Rueben, and Norman Shawchuck. *A Guide to Prayer for All Who Seek God*. Nashville, TN: Upper Room, 2006.

Keating, Thomas. *Active Meditations for Contemplative Prayer*. New York: Continuum, 1997.

———. *Foundations for Centering Prayer and the Christian Contemplative Life: Open Mind, Open Heart; Invitation to Love; The Mystery of Christ*. New York: Continuum, 2002.

Lewis, C.S. *Letters to Malcolm: Chiefly on Prayer*. New York and London: Harcourt Brace Jovanovich, 1964.

Merton, Thomas. *Contemplative Prayer*. New York: Herder and Herder, 1969.

Murray, Andrew. *With Christ in the School of Prayer*. Springdale, PA: Whitaker House, 1981.

Nouwen, Henri J. M. *With Open Hands*. Notre Dame, IN: Ave Maria Press, 1972.

———. *The Beauty of the Lord: Praying with Icons*. Notre Dame, IN: Ave Maria Press, 1987.

Rohr, Richard. *Everything Belongs: The Gift of Contemplative Prayer:* New York: Crossroads, 2003

Teresa of Avila. *A Life of Prayer*. Edited by Clayton Burg and James M. Houston. Colorado Springs, CO: David C. Cook Publishers, 2005.

Tickle, Phyllis. *The Divine Hours: Prayers for Autumn and Wintertime*. New York: Random House. 2000.

Ware, Timothy. ed. *The Art of Prayer: An Orthodox Anthology*. Translated by E. Kadloubovsky and E. M. Palmer. London: Faber and Faber, 1997.

Whyte, Alexander. *Lord, Teach Us To Pray*. Grand Rapids, MI, and Choteau, MT: Baker/Gospel Mission, 1976.

Willard, Dallas. *Hearing God: Developing a Conversational Relationship with God*. Downers Grove, IL: InterVarsity Press, 1999.

Relationship and Communion with God

Anonymous. *The Cloud of Unknowing*. San Francisco: Harper, 2004.

Bernard of Clairvaux. *The Love of God*. Edited by James M. Houston. Portland, OR: Multnomah Press, 1983.

Cornick, David. *Letting God Be God: The Reformed Tradition*. Maryknoll, NY: Orbis Books, 2008.

Davis, Ellen. *Getting Involved with God: Rediscovering the Old Testament.* Plymouth, United Kingdom: Cowley Publishers, 2001.

Edwards, Jonathan. *Religious Affections: A Christian's Character Before God.* Edited by James M. Houston. Minneapolis: Bethany House Publishers, 1996.

Foster, Richard J., and Gayle D. Beebe. *Longing for God: Seven Paths of Christian Devotion.* Downers Grove, IL: InterVarsity Press, 2009.

Garrison, J. H., and Gary Holloway. *Alone with God: A Manual of Devotions.* Siloam Springs, AR: Leafwood, 2003.

Guyon, Jeanne. *Experiencing the Depths of Jesus Christ.* Auburn, MA: Christian Books Publishing House, 1975.

Kempis, Thomas à. *The Imitation of Christ: How Jesus Wants Us to Live.* Translated by William Griffin. First edition. San Francisco: HarperSanFrancisco, 2000.

Manning, Brennan. *The Ragamuffin Gospel: Good News for the Bedraggled, Beat-Up, and Burnt Out.* Sisters, OR: Multnomah Books, 2005.

Owen, John. *Communion with God.* Abridged by R. J. K. Law. Edinburgh and Carlisle, PA: Banner of Truth Trust, 1991.

Palmer, Parker. *A Hidden Wholeness: The Journey Toward an Undivided Life.* San Francisco: Jossey-Bass, 2004.

Randall, Ian. *What a Friend We Have in Jesus: The Evangelical Tradition.* London: Darton, Longman, and Todd, 2005.

Rushing, Richard. *Voices From The Past: Puritan Devotional Readings.* Reprint edition. Edinburgh: Banner of Truth, 2009.

Tozer, A. W. *Keys to the Deeper Life.* Revised and expanded. Clarion Classics. Grand Rapids, MI: Zondervan, 1988.

———. *The Pursuit of God.* Camp Hill, PA: Christian Publications, 1993.

Webber, Robert. *The Divine Embrace: Recovering the Passionate Spiritual Life.* Grand Rapids, MI: Baker Books, 2006.

Willard, Dallas. *The Divine Conspiracy: Rediscovering Our Hidden Life in God.* First edition. San Francisco: HarperSanFrancisco, 1998.

———. *Renovation of the Heart: Putting on the Character of Christ.* Colorado Springs, CO: NavPress, 2002.

Spiritual Community

Allen, Holly Catterton. *Intergenerational Christian Formation: Bringing the Whole Church Together in Ministry, Community, and Worship.* Downers Grove, IL: IVP Academic, 2012.

Bonhoeffer, Dietrich. *Life Together.* San Francisco: HarperCollins, 1954.

Carlson, Kent, and Mike Lueken. *Renovation of the Church.* Downers Grove, IL: InterVarsity Press, 2011.

Morden, Peter J. *'Communion with Christ and His People': The Spirituality of C. H. Spurgeon.* Center for Baptist History and Heritage Studies, Volume 5. Oxford: Regent Park College, 2010.

Pettit, Paul, ed. *Foundations of Spiritual Formation: A Community Approach to Becoming Like Christ.* Grand Rapids, MI: Kregel Publications, 2008.

Scandrette, Mark. *Practicing the Way of Jesus: Life Together in the Kingdom of Love.* Downers Grove, IL: IVP Books, 2011.

Spiritual Disciplines

Augustine. *Confessions.* Translated and introduction by R. S. Pine-Coffin. London: Penguin Books, 1961.

Barton, Ruth Haley. *Invitation to Solitude and Silence: Experiencing God's Transforming Presence.* Expanded edition. Downers Grove, IL: IVP, 2010

Bass, Dorothy. *Practicing Our Faith: A Way of Life for a Searching People.* San Francisco: Jossey-Bass, 2010.

Benson, Bob, and Michael W. Benson. *Disciplines for the Inner Life.* Revised edition. Nashville, TN: Generoux/Nelson, 1989.

Brother Lawrence. *The Practice of the Presence of God.* New Kensington, PA: Whitaker House, 1982.

Calhoun, Adele Ahlberg. *Spiritual Disciplines Handbook: Practices That Transform Us.* Downers Grove, IL: InterVarsity Press, 2005.

Caussade, Jean Pierre de. *The Sacrament of the Present Moment.* First Harper & Row paperback edition. San Francisco: Harper & Row, 1982.

Caussade, Jean Pierre de. *Abandonment to Divine Providence: With Letters of Father De Caussade on the Practice of Self-Abandonment*. San Francisco, CA: Ignatius Press, 2011.

Chase, Steven. *Nature as Spiritual Practice*. New York: Eerdmans, 2011.

Chittister, Joan. *Wisdom Distilled from the Daily: Living the Rule of St. Benedict Today*. San Francisco: Harper, 1991.

De Wall, Esther. *The Way of Simplicity: The Cistercian Tradition*. Traditions of Christian Spirituality Series. New York: Orbis Books, 1998

Doherty, Catherine de Hueck. *Poustina: Christian Spirituality of the East for Western Man*. Notre Dame, IN: Ave Maria Press, 1975.

Edwards, Tilden. *Living in the Presence: Spiritual Exercises to Open Your Life to the Awareness of God*. San Francisco: HarperSanFrancisco, 1994.

Foster, Richard J. *Celebration of Discipline: The Path to Spiritual Growth*. 20th anniversary edition, Third edition. Revised edition. San Francisco: HarperSanFrancisco, 1998.

Foster, Richard J., and Emilie Griffin, eds. *Spiritual Classics: Selected Readings for Individuals and Groups on the Twelve Spiritual Disciplines*. First edition. San Francisco: HarperSanFrancisco, 2000.

Gross, Bobby. *Living the Christian Year: Time to Inhabit the Story of God*. Downers Grove, IL: InterVarsity Press, 2009.

Guenther, Margaret. *Holy Listening: The Art of Spiritual Direction*. Boston, MA: Cowley, 1992.

Hall, Thelma. *Too Deep for Words: Rediscovering Lectio Divina*. New York: Paulist, 1998.

Hudson, Trevor. *Discovering Our Spiritual Identity: Practices for God's Beloved*. Downers Grove, IL: InterVarsity Press, 2010.

Ignatius, and George E. Ganss. *Ignatius of Loyola: The Spiritual Exercises and Selected Works*. New York: Paulist Press, 1991.

Ireton, Kimberlee Conway. *The Circle of Seasons: Meeting God in the Church Year*. Downers Grove, IL: InterVarsity Press, 2008.

Jones, Tony. *The Sacred Way: Spiritual Practices for Everyday Life*. Grand Rapids, MI: Zondervan, 2004.

Kierkegaard, Søren. *Purity of Heart Is to Will One Thing: Spiritual Preparation for the Office of Confession*. Translated by Douglas V. Steere. New York: Harper, 1956.

Laird, Martin. *Into the Silent Land: A Guide to the Christian Practice of Contemplation.* Oxford, UK: Oxford, 2006.

Maas, Robin, and Gabriel O'Donnell, eds. *Spiritual Traditions for the Contemporary Church.* Nashville, TN: Abingdon Press, 1990.

Mulholland, M. Robert. *The Deeper Journey: The Spirituality of Discovering Your True Self.* Downers Grove, IL: InterVarsity Press, 2006.

Murray, Andrew. *Absolute Surrender: And Other Addresses.* Hall of Faith Classics 4. New York: G.I.L. Publications, 2015.

Nouwen, Henri J. M. *With Open Hands.* Notre Dame, IN: Ave Maria Press, 1972.

Ortberg, John. *The Life You've Always Wanted.* Philadelphia: Running Press, 2004.

Peterson, David. *Possessed by God: A New Testament Theology of Sanctification and Holiness.* New Studies in Biblical Theology 1. Leicester, England, and Downers Grove, IL: Apollos and InterVarsity Press, 1995.

Schwanda, Tom. "'Hearts Sweetly Refreshed': Puritan Spiritual Practices Then and Now." *Journal of Spiritual Formation and Soul Care* 3, no. 1 (Spring 2010): 21–41.

Steere, Douglas V. *Together in Solitude.* New York: Crossroad, 1982.

Whitney, Donald S. *Spiritual Disciplines for the Christian Life.* Colorado Springs, CO: NavPress, 1997.

Willard, Dallas. *The Spirit of the Disciplines: Understanding How God Changes Lives.* First edition. San Francisco: Harper & Row, 1988.

Spiritual Formation

Allen, Holly Catterton, ed. *Nurturing Children's Spirituality: Christian Perspectives and Best Practices.* Eugene, OR: Cascade Books, 2008.

Anderson, Fil. *Running on Empty: Contemplative Spirituality for Overachievers.* First edition. Colorado Springs, CO: WaterBrook Press, 2004.

Andrews, Alan, ed. *The Kingdom Life: A Practical Theology of Discipleship and Spiritual Formation.* Colorado Springs, CO: NavPress, 2010.

Anthony, Michael J., ed. *Perspectives on Children's Spiritual Formation: Four Views*. Nashville, TN: B&H Academic, 2006.

Boa, Kenneth. *Conformed to His Image: Biblical and Practical Approaches to Spiritual Formation*. Grand Rapids, MI: Zondervan, 2001.

Bushnell, Horace. *Christian Nurture.* New Haven, CT: Yale, 1861.

DeSilva, David. *Sacramental Life: Spiritual Formation Through the Book of Common Prayer*. Downers Grove, IL: InterVarsity Press, 2008.

Dowling, Elizabeth M., and W. George Scarlett, eds. *Encyclopedia of Religious and Spiritual Development*. Thousand Oaks, CA: SAGE Publications, 2006.

Fowler, James W. *Stages of Faith: The Psychology of Human Development and the Quest for Meaning*. First edition. San Francisco: Harper & Row, 1981.

Gire, Ken. *Windows of the Soul*. Grand Rapids, MI: Zondervan, 1996.

Greenman, Jeffrey P., and George Kalantzis, eds. *Life in the Spirit: Spiritual Formation in Theological Perspective*. Downers Grove, IL: IVP Academic, 2010.

Hagberg, Janet, and Robert A. Guelich. *The Critical Journey: Stages in the Life of Faith*. Salem, WI: Sheffield Publishing Co., 1995.

Holloway, Gary, and Earl Lavender. *Living God's Love: An Invitation to Christian Spirituality*. Siloam Springs, AR: Leafwood Pub, 2004.

Kelly, Thomas R. *A Testament of Devotion*. San Francisco: HarperSanFrancisco, 1996.

Mulholland, M. Robert. *Invitation to a Journey: A Road Map for Spiritual Formation*. Downers Grove, IL: InterVarsity, 1993.

———. *The Deeper Journey: The Spirituality of Discovering Your True Self*. Downers Grove, IL: InterVarsity Press, 2006.

Nouwen, Henri J. M. *With Open Hands*. Notre Dame, IN: Ave Maria Press, 1972.

———. *The Genesee Diary*. Garden City, NY: Image Books, 1976.

———. *Making All Things New: An Invitation to the Spiritual Life*. First edition. San Francisco: Harper & Row, 1981.

———. *The Way of the Heart: Desert Spirituality and Contemporary Ministry*. New York: Seabury, 1981.

———. *Reaching Out: The Three Movements of the Spiritual Life*. Garden City, NY: Image Books, 1986.

———. *The Beauty of the Lord: Praying with Icons.* Notre Dame, IN: Ave Maria Press, 1987.

———. *In the Name of Jesus: Reflections on Christian Leadership.* New York: Crossroad, 1989.

———. *Life of the Beloved: Spiritual Living in a Secular World.* New York: Crossroad, 1992.

———. *Ministry and Spirituality.* Revised and compiled edition. New York: Continuum, 1996.

———. *Out of Solitude: Three Meditations on the Christian Life.* First revised edition. Notre Dame, IN: Ave Maria Press, 2004.

Parrett, Gary A., and S. Steve Kang. *Teaching the Faith, Forming the Faithful: A Biblical Vision for Education in the Church.* Downers Grove, IL: IVP Academic, 2009.

Pettit, Paul, ed. *Foundations of Spiritual Formation: A Community Approach to Becoming Like Christ.* Grand Rapids, MI: Kregel Publications, 2008.

Sales, Francis de. *Introduction to the Devout Life.* New York: Vintage Books, 2002.

Scandrette, Mark. *Practicing the Way of Jesus: Life Together in the Kingdom of Love.* Downers Grove, IL: IVP Books, 2011.

Scazzero, Peter. *Emotionally Healthy Spirituality: Unleash a Revolution in Your Life in Christ.* Nashville, TN: Integrity, 2006.

Spiritual Formation Training, Journal of Psychology & Christianity 32, no. 4 (December 2013).

Taylor-Stinson, Therese. "Black Spirituality and the Art of Spiritual Direction." *Presence: An International Journal of Spiritual Direction* 15, no. 4 (December 2009): 46–55.

Thompson, Marjorie J. *Soul Feast: An Invitation to the Christian Spiritual Life.* Louisville, KY: Westminster John Knox Press, 2005.

Tippens, Darryl. *Pilgrim Heart: The Way of Jesus in Everyday Life.* Abilene, TX: Leafwood Publishers, 2006.

Underhill, Evelyn. *The Spiritual Life.* Harrisburg, PA: Morehouse Publishing, 1991.

Waggoner, Brad J. *The Shape of Faith to Come: Spiritual Formation and the Future of Discipleship.* Nashville, TN: B&H Publishing Group, 2008.

Whitney, Donald S. *Ten Questions to Diagnose Your Spiritual Health*. Colorado Springs, CO: NavPress, 2001.

Wilhoit, James C. *Spiritual Formation as If the Church Mattered: Growing in Christ Through Community*. Grand Rapids, MI: Baker Academic, 2008.

Willard, Dallas. *The Divine Conspiracy: Rediscovering Our Hidden Life in God*. First edition. San Francisco: HarperSanFrancisco, 1998.

———. *Renovation of the Heart: Putting on the Character of Christ*. Colorado Springs, CO: NavPress, 2002.

The Living Word

Bartlett, David L., and Barbra Brown Taylor, eds. *Feasting on the Word: Preaching the Revised Common Lectionary*. Louisville, KY: Westminster John Knox, 2011.

Mulholland, M. Robert. *Shaped by the Word: The Power of Scripture in Spiritual Formation*. Revised edition. Nashville, TN: Upper Room Books, 2000.

Theology

Allen, Diogenes. *Spiritual Theology: The Theology of Yesterday for Spiritual Help Today*. Cambridge, MA: Cowley Publications, 1997.

Andrews, Alan, ed. *The Kingdom Life: A Practical Theology of Discipleship and Spiritual Formation*. Colorado Springs, CO: NavPress, 2010.

Balswick, Jack O., Pamela Ebstyne King, and Kevin S. Reimer. *The Reciprocating Self: Human Development in Theological Perspective*. Downers Grove, IL: InterVarsity Press, 2005.

Chan, Simon. *Spiritual Theology: A Systematic Study of the Christian Life*. Downers Grove, IL: InterVarsity Press, 1998.

———. *Pentecostal Theology and the Christian Spiritual Tradition*. Sheffield, England: Sheffield Academic Press, 2000.

Christie, Douglas E. *The Blue Sapphire of the Mind: Notes for a Contemplative Ecology*. New York: Oxford University Press, 2012.

Estep, James Riley, and Jonathan H. Kim, eds. *Christian Formation: Integrating Theology & Human Development.* Nashville, TN: B&H Academic, 2010.

Greenman, Jeffrey P., and George Kalantzis, eds. *Life in the Spirit: Spiritual Formation in Theological Perspective.* Downers Grove, IL: IVP Academic, 2010.

Harrison, Nonna Verna. *God's Many-Splendored Image: Theological Anthropology for Christian Formation.* Grand Rapids, MI: Baker Academic, 2010.

Jones, Cheslyn, Geoffrey Wainwright, and Edward Yarnold, eds. *The Study of Spirituality.* New York: Oxford University Press, 1986.

Lindberg, Carter, ed. *The Pietist Theologians.* Malden, MA: Blackwell Publishing, 2005.

Peterson, David. *Possessed by God: A New Testament Theology of Sanctification and Holiness.* New Studies in Biblical Theology 1. Leicester, England, and Downers Grove, IL: Apollos and InterVarsity Press, 1995.

Peterson, Eugene H. *Christ Plays in Ten Thousand Places: A Conversation in Spiritual Theology.* Grand Rapids, MI: W.B. Eerdmans, 2005.

Sheldrake, Philip F. *Explorations in Spirituality: History, Theology, and Social Practice.* Mahwah, NJ: Paulist Press, 2010.

Tozer, A. W. *The Knowledge of the Holy.* San Francisco: HarperSanFrancisco, 1961.

Tyson, John R. *Invitation to Christian Spirituality: An Ecumenical Anthology.* New York: Oxford University Press, 1999.

Wiseman, James A. *Spirituality and Mysticism: A Global View.* Maryknoll, NY: Orbis Books, 2006.

Appendix B

Not on Bread Alone Menu
(yearly Bible reading plan)

Our *Not On Break Alone (NOBA) Menu* is our yearly Bible reading plan. Our desire is for every member to read through God's Word each year. We believe that intentionally being in God's Word is a vital part of growing as a disciple of Christ. We call this a menu because we believe that intake of God's Word is as important (if not more important) than the intake of physical food.

The following pages include the full NOBA Menu. This plan is designed in such a way that an individual can join in the reading at any point in the year. This reading plan was designed by The Navigators[1] and is called the Discipleship Journal Reading Plan with some adaptation on our part. It takes you to four separate places in Scripture each day to help you better understand the unity of God's Word in the midst of four differing viewpoints. It is also designed to help you not fall too far behind by scheduling 25 days of reading each month. This leaves you with five to six "free days" to either catch up or to read further on your own. Now, go and feast!

---

1. For more information, go to www.navigators.org and click on tools to find this Bible reading plan.

JANUARY

Day	✔	New Testament MATTHEW	New Testament ACTS	Old Testament PSALMS	Old Testament EXODUS
1		10:21–42	15:22–41	24	1–3
2		11:1–19	16:1–15	25	4–6
3		11:20–30	16:16–40	26	7–9
4		12:1–21	17:1–15	27	10–12
5		12:22–37	17:16–34	28	13–15
6		12:38–50	18:1–17	29	16–18
7		13:1–23	18:18–28	30	19–20
8		13:24–43	19:1–22	31	21–23
9		13:44–58	19:23–41	32	24–26
10		14:1–21	20:1–12	33	27–29
11		14:22–36	20:13–38	34	30–31
12		15:1–20	21:1–26	35	32–33
13		15:21–39	21:27–40	36	34
14		16:1–12	22	37:1–22	35–37
15		16:13–28	23:1–11	37:23–40	38–40
					LEVITICUS
16		17:1–13	23:12–35	38	1–4
17		17:14–27	24	39	5–7
18		18:1–14	25:1–12	40	8–10
19		18:15–35	25:13–27	41	11–13
20		19:1–15	26:1–18	42	14–15
21		19:16–30	26:19–32	43	16–17
22		20:1–16	27:1–26	44	18–20
23		20:17–34	27:27–44	45	21–23
24		21:1–11	28:1–16	46	24–25
25		21:12–22	28:17–31	47	26–27

FEBRUARY

Day	✔	New Testament MATTHEW	New Testament ROMANS	Old Testament PSALMS	Old Testament NUMBERS
1		21:23–32	1:1–17	48	1–2
2		21:33–46	1:18–32	49	3–4
3		22:1–14	2	50	5–6
4		22:15–33	3	51	7–8
5		22:34–46	4	52	9–11
6		23:1–12	5:1–11	53	12–14
7		23:13–24	5:12–21	54	15–17
8		23:25–39	6:1–14	55	18–20
9		24:1–14	6:15–23	56	21–22
10		24:15–35	7:1–12	57	23–25
11		24:36–51	7:13–25	58	26–27
12		25:1–13	8:1–17	59	28–30
13		25:14–30	8:18–39	60	31–32
14		25:31–46	9:1–18	61	33–36
					DEUTERONOMY
15		26:1–16	9:19–33	62	1–3
16		26:17–35	10	63	4–5
17		26:36–56	11:1–24	64	6–8
18		26:57–75	11:25–36	65	9–12
19		27:1–10	12:1–8	66	13–17
20		27:11–26	12:9–21	67	18–21
21		27:27–44	13	68	22–26
22		27:45–56	14	69:1–18	27–28
23		27:57–66	15:1–13	69:19–36	29–31
24		28:1–10	15:14–33	70	32
25		28:11–20	16	71	33–34

MARCH

Day	✔	MARK (New Testament)	I CORINTHIANS (New Testament)	PSALMS (Old Testament)	JOSHUA (Old Testament)
1		1:1–8	1:1–17	72	1–2
2		1:9–20	1:18–31	73	3–5
3		1:21–34	2	74	6–7
4		1:35–45	3	75	8–9
5		2:1–12	4	76	10–12
6		2:13–17	5	77	13–14
7		2:18–28	6:1–11	78:1–39	15–17
8		3:1–19	6:12–20	78:40–72	18–19
9		3:20–35	7:1–16	79	20–21
10		4:1–20	7:17–40	80	22–23
11		4:21–41	8	81	24
					JUDGES
12		5:1–20	9:1–12	82	1–3
13		5:21–43	9:13–27	83	4–5
14		6:1–13	10:1–13	84	6–7
15		6:14–29	10:14–33	85	8
16		6:30–44	11:1–16	86	9
17		6:45–56	11:17–34	87	10–12
18		7:1–23	12:1–13	88	13–15
19		7:24–37	12:14–31	89:1–18	16
20		8:1–13	13	89:19–52	17–18
21		8:14–21	14:1–25	90	19
22		8:22–30	14:26–40	91	20–21
					RUTH
23		8:31–38	15:1–28	92	1
24		9:1–13	15:29–58	93	2–3
25		9:14–32	16	94	4

APRIL

Day	✔	New Testament MARK	New Testament 2 CORINTHIANS	Old Testament PSALMS	Old Testament 1 SAMUEL
1		9:33–50	1:1–11	95	1–2
2		10:1–16	1:12–24	96	3–5
3		10:17–34	2	97	6–8
4		10:35–52	3	98	9–10
5		11:1–11	4	99	11–13
6		11:12–26	5	100	14
7		11:27–33	6	101	15–16
8		12:1–12	7	102	17–18
9		12:13–27	8	103	19–20
10		12:28–34	9	104	21–23
11		12:35–44	10	105	24–25
12		13:1–13	11:1–15	106:1–23	26–28
13		13:14–31	11:16–33	106:24–48	29–31
					2 SAMUEL
14		13:32–37	12:1–10	107	1–2
15		14:1–11	12:11–21	108	3–4
16		14:12–31	13	109	5–7
			GALATIANS		
17		14:32–42	1	110	8–10
18		14:43–52	2	111	11–12
19		14:53–65	3:1–14	112	13
20		14:66–72	3:15–29	113	14–15
21		15:1–15	4:1–20	114	16–17
22		15:16–32	4:21–31	115	18–19
23		15:33–41	5:1–12	116	20–21
24		15:42–47	5:13–26	117	22
25		16	6	118	23–24

MAY

Day	✔	New Testament		Old Testament	
		LUKE	EPHESIANS	PSALMS	1 KINGS
1		1:1–25	1:1–14	119:1–8	1
2		1:26–38	1:15–23	119:9–16	2–3
3		1:39–56	2:1–10	119:17–24	4–5
4		1:57–66	2:11–22	119:25–32	6–7
5		1:67–80	3:1–13	119:33–40	8
6		2:1–20	3:14–21	119:41–48	9–10
7		2:21–40	4:1–16	119:49–56	11
8		2:41–52	4:17–24	119:57–64	12
9		3:1–20	4:25–32	119:65–72	13–14
10		3:21–38	5:1–21	119:73–80	15–16
11		4:1–12	5:22–33	119:81–88	17–18
12		4:13–30	6:1–9	119:89–96	19–20
13		4:31–37	6:10–24	119:97–104	21–22
					2 KINGS
14		4:38–44	1:1–11	119:105–112	1–3
15		5:1–11	1:12–20	119:113–120	4–5
16		5:12–16	1:21–30	119:121–128	6–7
17		5:17–26	2:1–11	119:129–136	8–9
18		5:27–32	2:12–18	119:137–144	10–11
19		5:33–39	2:19–30	119:145–152	12–13
20		6:1–16	3:1–9	119:153–160	14–15
21		6:17–26	3:10–14	119:161–168	16–17
22		6:27–36	3:15–21	119:169–176	18–19
23		6:37–42	4:1–7	120	20–21
24		6:43–49	4:8–13	121	22–23
25		7:1–10	4:14–23	122	24–25

JUNE

Day	✔	New Testament LUKE	New Testament COLOSSIANS	Old Testament PSALMS	Old Testament 1 CHRONICLES
1		7:11–17	1:1–14	123–124	1–2
2		7:18–35	1:15–29	125	3–4
3		7:36–50	2:1–7	126	5–6
4		8:1–15	2:8–15	127	7–9
5		8:16–25	2:16–23	128	10–11
6		8:26–39	3:1–14	129	12–14
7		8:40–56	3:15–25	130–131	15–16
8		9:1–17	4:1–9	132	17–19
9		9:18–27	4:10–18	133–134	20–22
			1 THESSALONIANS		
10		9:28–36	1	135	23–25
11		9:37–50	2:1–9	136	26–28
12		9:51–62	2:10–20	137	29
					2 CHRONICLES
13		10:1–16	3:1–6	138	1–2
14		10:17–24	3:7–13	139	3–5
15		10:25–37	4:1–10	140	6–7
16		10:38–42	4:11–18	141	8–9
17		11:1–13	5:1–11	142	10–12
18		11:14–28	5:12–28	143	13–16
			2 THESSALONIANS		
19		11:29–36	1:1–7	144	17–19
20		11:37–54	1:8–12	145	20–21
21		12:1–12	2:1–12	146	22–24
22		12:13–21	2:13–17	147	25–27
23		12:22–34	3:1–5	148	28–29
24		12:35–48	3:6–13	149	30–33
25		12:49–59	3:14–18	150	34–36

JULY

Day	✔	New Testament		Old Testament	
		LUKE	1 TIMOTHY	PROVERBS	EZRA
1		13:1–9	1:1–11	1	1–2
2		13:10–21	1:12–20	2	3
3		13:22–35	2	3	4–5
4		14:1–14	3:1–10	4	6
5		14:15–24	3:11–16	5	7
6		14:25–35	4	6	8
7		15:1–10	5:1–15	7	9
8		15:11–32	5:16–25	8	10
					NEHEMIAH
9		16:1–9	6:1–10	9	1–2
10		16:10–18	6:11–21	10:1–16	3
			2 TIMOTHY		
11		16:19–31	1:1–7	10:17–32	4–5
12		17:1–10	1:8–18	11:1–15	6
13		17:11–19	2:1–13	11:16–31	7
14		17:20–37	2:14–26	12:1–14	8
15		18:1–8	3:1–9	12:15–28	9
16		18:9–17	3:10–17	13:1–12	10
17		18:18–30	4	13:13–25	11
			TITUS		
18		18:31–43	1:1–9	14:1–18	12
19		19:1–10	1:10–16	14:19–35	13
					ESTHER
20		19:11–27	2:1–10	15:1–17	1
21		19:28–38	2:11–15	15:18–33	2
22		19:39–48	3:1–8	16:1–16	3–4
23		20:1–8	3:9–15	16:17–33	5–6
			PHILEMON		
24		20:9–19	1–11	17:1–14	7–8
25		20:20–26	12–25	17:15–28	9–10

AUGUST

Day	✔	New Testament LUKE	New Testament HEBREWS	Old Testament PROVERBS	Old Testament ISAIAH
1		20:27–40	1:1–9	18	1–2
2		20:41–47	1:10–14	19:1–14	3–5
3		21:1–19	2:1–9	19:15–29	6–8
4		21:20–28	2:10–18	20:1–15	9–10
5		21:29–38	3	20:16–30	11–13
6		22:1–13	4:1–11	21:1–16	14–16
7		22:14–23	4:12–16	21:17–31	17–20
8		22:24–30	5	22:1–16	21–23
9		22:31–38	6:1–12	22:17–29	24–26
10		22:39–46	6:13–20	23:1–18	27–28
11		22:47–53	7:1–10	23:19–35	29–30
12		22:54–62	7:11–28	24:1–22	31–33
13		22:63–71	8:1–6	24:23–34	34–36
14		23:1–12	8:7–13	25:1–14	37–39
15		23:13–25	9:1–10	25:15–28	40–41
16		23:26–31	9:11–28	26:1–16	42–43
17		23:32–37	10:1–18	26:17–28	44–45
18		23:38–43	10:19–39	27:1–14	46–48
19		23:44–49	11:1–16	27:15–27	49–50
20		23:50–56	11:17–31	28:1–14	51–53
21		24:1–12	11:32–40	28:15–28	54–55
22		24:13–27	12:1–13	29:1–14	56–58
23		24:28–35	12:14–29	29:15–27	59–61
24		24:36–44	13:1–8	30	62–64
25		24:45–53	13:9–25	31	65–66

SEPTEMBER

Day	✔	New Testament JOHN	New Testament JAMES	Old Testament ECCLESIASTES	Old Testament JEREMIAH
1		1:1–18	1:1–11	1	1–2
2		1:19–28	1:12–18	2:1–16	3–4
3		1:29–34	1:19–27	2:17–26	5–6
4		1:35–42	2:1–13	3:1–15	7–9
5		1:43–51	2:14–26	3:16–22	10–11
6		2:1–11	3:1–12	4	12–13
7		2:12–25	3:13–18	5	14–15
8		3:1–15	4:1–10	6	16–18
9		3:16–21	4:11–17	7:1–14	19–22
10		3:22–36	5:1–6	7:15–29	23–25
11		4:1–14	5:7–12	8	26–29
12		4:15–26	5:13–20	9	30–31
			1 PETER		
13		4:27–42	1:1–9	10	32–34
14		4:43–54	1:10–16	11	35–38
15		5:1–15	1:17–25	12	39–43
				SONG OF SONGS	
16		5:16–30	2:1–8	1	44–46
17		5:31–47	2:9–17	2	47–48
18		6:1–15	2:18–25	3	49
19		6:16–24	3:1–7	4:1–7	50
20		6:25–40	3:8–12	4:8–16	51
21		6:41–59	3:13–22	5	52
					LAMENTATIONS
22		6:60–71	4:1–11	6	1
23		7:1–13	4:12–19	7	2
24		7:14–24	5:1–7	8:1–7	3
25		7:25–36	5:8–14	8:8–14	4–5

OCTOBER

Day	✔	New Testament JOHN	New Testament 2 PETER	Old Testament JOB	Old Testament EZEKIEL
1		7:37–44	1:1–11	1	1–3
2		7:45–53	1:12–21	2	4–8
3		8:1–11	2:1–9	3	9–12
4		8:12–20	2:10–16	4	13–15
5		8:21–30	2:17–22	5	16
6		8:31–47	3:1–9	6	17–19
7		8:48–59	3:10–18	7	20–21
			1 JOHN		
8		9:1–12	1:1–4	8	22–23
9		9:13–25	1:5–10	9:1–20	24–26
10		9:26–41	2:1–11	9:21–35	27–28
11		10:1–10	2:12–17	10	29–30
12		10:11–21	2:18–23	11	31–32
13		10:22–42	2:24–29	12	33–34
14		11:1–16	3:1–10	13	35–37
15		11:17–37	3:11–18	14	38–39
16		11:38–44	3:19–24	15:1–16	40–41
17		11:45–57	4:1–6	15:17–35	42–44
18		12:1–11	4:7–21	16	45–47
19		12:12–19	5:1–12	17	48
					DANIEL
20		12:20–36	5:13–21	18	1–2
			2 JOHN		
21		12:37–50	1–13	19	3–4
			3 JOHN		
22		13:1–11	1–14	20	5–6
			JUDE		
23		13:12–17	1–7	21:1–21	7–8
24		13:18–30	8–16	21:22–34	9
25		13:31–38	17–25	22	10–12

NOVEMBER

Day	✔	New Testament JOHN	New Testament REVELATION	Old Testament JOB	Old Testament HOSEA
1		14:1–14	1:1–8	23	1–3
2		14:15–21	1:9–20	24	4–6
3		14:22–31	2:1–17	25–26	7–8
4		15:1–8	2:18–29	27	9–12
5		15:9–17	3:1–13	28	13–14
					JOEL
6		15:18–27	3:14–22	29	1
7		16:1–11	4	30	2–3
					AMOS
8		16:12–24	5	31:1–23	1–2
9		16:25–33	6	31:24–40	3–4
10		17:1–5	7	32	5–6
11		17:6–19	8	33:1–11	7–9
					OBADIAH
12		17:20–26	9	33:12–33	1–21
					JONAH
13		18:1–18	10	34:1–20	1–4
					MICAH
14		18:19–27	11	34:21–37	1–3
15		18:28–40	12	35	4–5
16		19:1–16	13	36:1–15	6–7
					NAHUM
17		19:17–27	14	36:16–33	1–3
					HABAKKUK
18		19:28–37	15	37	1–3
					ZEPHANIAH
19		19:38–42	16	38:1–21	1–2
20		20:1–9	17	38:22–41	3
					HAGGAI
21		20:10–18	18	39	1–2
					ZECHARIAH
22		20:19–23	19	40	1–5
23		20:24–31	20	41:1–11	6–9
24		21:1–14	21	41:12–34	10–14
					MALACHI
25		21:15–25	22	42	1–4

DECEMBER

Day	✔	New Testament		Old Testament	
		MATTHEW	ACTS	PSALMS	GENESIS
1		1:1–17	1:1–11	1	1–2
2		1:18–25	1:12–26	2	3–4
3		2:1–12	2:1–21	3	5–8
4		2:13–23	2:22–47	4	9–11
5		3:1–12	3	5	12–14
6		3:13–17	4:1–22	6	15–17
7		4:1–11	4:23–37	7	18–20
8		4:12–17	5:1–16	8	21–23
9		4:18–25	5:17–42	9	24
10		5:1–12	6	10	25–26
11		5:13–20	7:1–38	11	27–28
12		5:21–32	7:39–60	12	29–30
13		5:33–48	8:1–25	13	31
14		6:1–15	8:26–40	14	32–33
15		6:16–24	9:1–19	15	34–35
16		6:25–34	9:20–43	16	36
17		7:1–14	10:1–23	17	37–38
18		7:15–29	10:24–48	18:1–24	39–40
19		8:1–13	11:1–18	18:25–50	41
20		8:14–22	11:19–30	19	42–43
21		8:23–34	12	20	44–45
22		9:1–13	13:1–25	21	46–47
23		9:14–26	13:26–52	22:1–11	48
24		9:27–38	14	22:12–31	49
25		10:1–20	15:1–21	23	50

Appendix C

Six-Year Scope and Sequence
(curriculum plan)

We believe that Bible study in the midst of other believers is a vital part of our spiritual formation and discipleship. Therefore, we ask that all our members regularly take part in a Sunday morning Bible class to explore God's Word with other brothers and sisters in Christ so that mutual growth can take place.

The following is our coordinated 6-Year Scope and Sequence plan for Bible classes. As mentioned earlier, this 6-year curriculum aligns with the Not On Bread Alone yearly reading plan found in Appendix B. That way, you will be reading in the areas of Scripture that will be taught in Bible classes for children youth, and adult studies.

Our hope is to approach our formation as disciples holistically so that we may have common conversations about God's Word and what it is revealing to us at any given time of the year with any given group or individual in the church family. We hope that the NOBA Menu and 6-year curriculum provides guidance for the study of Scripture from individual (personal Bible study and devotion), to group (Bible classes, study groups, discipleship groups), to congregational (sermons, growth groups) perspectives. It thus provides us with a common place to come together in our spiritual growth and nurturance.

YEAR 1

Fall Semester

Area	Approach	Audience
Textual: NT	James	Mixed
Textual: OT	Exodus/Numbers	Mixed
Training	Foundations: Christian Beliefs	New Converts
Training	Covered in Dust: Discipleship Training	Mixed
Topical	Why? The Demanding Questions of Life	Mixed
Topical	Loving God/Loving Others: A Study of God's Love & Grace	Mixed
Topical	OPEN APPROACH	OPEN AUDIENCE

Spring Semester

Area	Approach	Audience
Textual: NT	Matthew	Mixed
Textual: OT	Joshua	Mixed
Training	Outreach/Evangelism Training	Mixed
Topical	Forgiveness According to God	Mixed
Topical	Modern Day Idols/Counterfeit Gods	Mixed
Topical	OPEN APPROACH	OPEN AUDIENCE
Topical	OPEN APPROACH	OPEN AUDIENCE

Maymester

ELDERS' CHOICE

Summer Semester

Area	Approach	Audience
Textual: NT	1 & 2 Thessalonians	Mixed
Textual: OT	Judges	Mixed
Training	Connecting with My FXCC Family	Mixed/Specific
Topical	Difficult Questions/Difficult Answers	Mixed
Topical	God and Finances	Mixed
Topical	OPEN APPROACH	OPEN AUDIENCE
Topical	OPEN APPROACH	OPEN AUDIENCE

YEAR 2

Fall Semester

Area	Approach	Audience
Textual: NT	1, 2, 3 John	Mixed
Textual: OT	Leviticus/Deuteronomy	Mixed
Training	Foundations: Christian Beliefs	New Converts
Training	Covered in Dust: Discipleship Training	Mixed
Topical	Addressing Cultural Issues	Mixed
Topical	Parenting by the Book	Mixed
Topical	OPEN APPROACH	OPEN AUDIENCE

Spring Semester

Area	Approach	Audience
Textual: NT	1 Corinthians	Mixed
Textual: OT	1 & 2 Samuel	Mixed
Training	Outreach/Evangelism Training	Mixed
Topical	Marriage by the Book	Mixed
Topical	What Is Truth? Christianity and Postmodern Thought	Mixed
Topical	OPEN APPROACH	OPEN AUDIENCE
Topical	OPEN APPROACH	OPEN AUDIENCE

Maymester

ELDERS' CHOICE

Summer Semester

Area	Approach	Audience
Textual: NT	Galatians	Mixed
Textual: OT	Psalms	Mixed
Training	Connecting with My FXCC Family	Mixed/Specific
Topical	As Iron Sharpens Iron: A Men's Study	Men All Ages
Topical	God's Word and How to Study It	Mixed
Topical	OPEN APPROACH	OPEN AUDIENCE
Topical	OPEN APPROACH	OPEN AUDIENCE

YEAR 3

Fall Semester

Area	Approach	Audience
Textual: NT	2 Corinthians	Mixed
Textual: OT	Kings & Chronicles	Mixed
Training	Foundations: Christian Beliefs	New Converts
Training	Covered in Dust: Discipleship Training	Mixed
Topical	Christian Apologetics	Mixed
Topical	God and Human Sexuality	Mixed
Topical	OPEN APPROACH	OPEN AUDIENCE

Spring Semester

Area	Approach	Audience
Textual: NT	Luke	Mixed
Textual: OT	Proverbs	Mixed
Training	Outreach/Evangelism Training	Mixed
Topical	Living the Spiritual Disciplines	Mixed
Topical	The Character of Christ: Christian Integrity in a Fallen World	Mixed
Topical	OPEN APPROACH	OPEN AUDIENCE
Topical	OPEN APPROACH	OPEN AUDIENCE

Maymester

ELDERS' CHOICE

Summer Semester

Area	Approach	Audience
Textual: NT	Romans	Mixed
Textual: OT	Ecclesiastes	Mixed
Training	Connecting with My FXCC Family	Mixed/Specific
Topical	Tackling Today's Hot Topics	Mixed
Topical	Having the Difficult Conversations with Your Kids	Mixed
Topical	OPEN APPROACH	OPEN AUDIENCE
Topical	OPEN APPROACH	OPEN AUDIENCE

YEAR 4

Fall Semester

Area	Approach	Audience
Textual: NT	Ephesians/Colossians	Mixed
Textual: OT	Minor Prophets	Mixed
Training	Foundations: Christian Beliefs	New Converts
Training	Covered in Dust: Discipleship Training	Mixed
Topical	Knowing and Being Known by God	Mixed
Topical	The Unseen Battle: Study on Spiritual Warfare	Mixed
Topical	OPEN APPROACH	OPEN AUDIENCE

Spring Semester

Area	Approach	Audience
Textual: NT	Mark	Mixed
Textual: OT	Isaiah	Mixed
Training	Outreach/Evangelism Training	Mixed
Topical	Pure Religion: God's Social Justice	Mixed
Topical	Redeeming Relationships: God's Plan for Relationships	Mixed
Topical	OPEN APPROACH	OPEN AUDIENCE
Topical	OPEN APPROACH	OPEN AUDIENCE

Maymester

ELDERS' CHOICE

Summer Semester

Area	Approach	Audience
Textual: NT	1 & 2 Timothy, Titus	Mixed
Textual: OT	Ezekiel/Daniel	Mixed
Training	Connecting with My FXCC Family	Mixed/Specific
Topical	The One Anothers: Unity	Mixed
Topical	Leading and Mentoring Like Jesus	Mixed
Topical	OPEN APPROACH	OPEN AUDIENCE
Topical	OPEN APPROACH	OPEN AUDIENCE

YEAR 5

Fall Semester

Area	Approach	Audience
Textual: NT	Philippians/Philemon	Mixed
Textual: OT	Ruth/Esther	Mixed
Training	Foundations: Christian Beliefs	New Converts
Training	Covered in Dust: Discipleship Training	Mixed
Topical	Great Themes in Scripture: Study in Systematic Theology	Mixed
Topical	Transformed Images: A Study of Spiritual Formation	Mixed
Topical	OPEN APPROACH	OPEN AUDIENCE

Spring Semester

Area	Approach	Audience
Textual: NT	1 & 2 Peter, Jude	Mixed
Textual: OT	Ezra/Nehemiah	Mixed
Training	Outreach/Evangelism Training	Mixed
Topical	God's Mission/Our Mission: God's Redemptive Plan and Our Part in It	Mixed
Topical	Prayer	Mixed
Topical	OPEN APPROACH	OPEN AUDIENCE
Topical	OPEN APPROACH	OPEN AUDIENCE

Maymester

ELDERS' CHOICE

Summer Semester

Area	Approach	Audience
Textual: NT	Hebrews	Mixed
Textual: OT	Jeremiah/Lamentations	Mixed
Training	Connecting with My FXCC Family	Mixed/Specific
Topical	Spiritual Maturity: Life After Kids and Into Retirement	Mixed
Topical	Church History and the Modern Church	Mixed
Topical	OPEN APPROACH	OPEN AUDIENCE
Topical	OPEN APPROACH	OPEN AUDIENCE

YEAR 6

Fall Semester

Area	Approach	Audience
Textual: NT	John	Mixed
Textual: OT	Genesis	Mixed
Training	Foundations: Christian Beliefs	New Converts
Training	Covered in Dust: Discipleship Training	Mixed
Topical	When Life Gets Hard: A Study of Living Through Suffering	Mixed
Topical	God and Science: For or Against?	Mixed
Topical	OPEN APPROACH	OPEN AUDIENCE

Spring Semester

Area	Approach	Audience
Textual: NT	Acts	Mixed
Textual: OT	Job	Mixed
Training	Outreach/Evangelism Training	Mixed
Topic	The Holy Spirit	Mixed
Topic	Addressing Cultural Issues	Mixed
Topic	OPEN APPROACH	OPEN AUDIENCE
Topical	OPEN APPROACH	OPEN AUDIENCE

Maymester

ELDERS' CHOICE

Summer Semester

Area	Approach	Audience
Textual: NT	Revelation	Mixed
Textual: OT	Song of Solomon	Mixed
Training	Connecting with My FXCC Family	Mixed/Specific
Topical	God's Story Through Scripture: Biblical Theology	Mixed
Topical	I'm Busy: How to Live for God in a Fast-Paced World	Mixed
Topical	OPEN APPROACH	OPEN AUDIENCE
Topical	OPEN APPROACH	OPEN AUDIENCE

Appendix D

Covered in Dust: A Journey in Discipleship

Covered in Dust is a curriculum that we designed to aid our discipleship groups in their journey in discipleship together. The title of this study, "Covered in Dust," is intended to communicate our desire to foster discipling relationships that are following Jesus so closely that He will cover us all with the dust of His feet. We want to follow Him so closely that we are covered with His words, actions, and attitudes and that we are "drinking in His words with thirst."

This study is designed to be an ongoing conversation during a year between two, three, or four individuals as they commit to one another to become committed disciples of Christ. True discipleship is mutual and relational in nature. Although one in the relationship may be more spiritually mature (by age or years in faith), we all are continual learners and are being discipled in Christ through the span of our lives.

This study assumes that the participants have already made a commitment to Christ and have been baptized. In other words, the go, make, and baptize of the Great Commission have been fulfilled in these individuals. We recognize that we are really good with having people make a commitment to Christ, but poor at helping them keep it.

"Covered in Dust" is designed to help people in their journey of discipleship after they make a commitment to Christ. In this journey, we will focus on becoming more like Christ by building relationships, meeting regularly, and holding each other accountable to the designed conversations together.

Please contact the church office at church.office@fxcc.org or 703-631-2100 to receive help on how to form a discipleship group and how to receive copies of the "Covered in Dust" curriculum.

Appendix E

What Our Family Believes

As a church family (a group of imperfect people seeking the Lord), we believe the Bible is God's message revealed to us for the purpose of guiding us toward Him. With this in mind, in the Bible (Hebrews 6:1–3) we find essential truths that lay the foundation for our faith in Jesus Christ. Those truths are at the core of who we are as a church:

- Our family believes in *one* eternal God, who is Father, Son, and Holy Spirit (Matthew 5:16, 5:45, 6:1, 6:4, 6:8–9; James 1:17; John 1:1, 14:9; Genesis 1:2; John 4:24, 14:16–20; 2 Peter 1:21)
  - Our family believes in *God the Father*, who is the Creator of all things seen and unseen. (Genesis 1:1; Acts 17:24–28; Hebrews 11:3)
  - Our family believes in *God the Son*, Jesus Christ, who is God's Son and our Savior (John 1:14; 1 John 4:9; John 3:16; 2 Peter 3:18) and who
    - Was born Jesus of Nazareth, both fully human and fully divine, conceived of the Holy Spirit and born of the virgin Mary. (Matthew 21:11; John 19:19; John 1:14; Romans 5:15–17; Colossians 2:9; 1 John 1:1; Matthew 1:18; Luke 1:26–38)
    - Lived and taught the perfect life. (John 13:14–16; Philippians 2:1–11; Hebrews 2:14–18, 3:1, 4:14–16, 12:1–3; 1 Peter 2:21; 1 John 2:6)

- Suffered and was unjustly crucified. (Luke 23:1–46)
- Died, was buried, and rose from the grave on the third day following His death. (Luke 23:44–24:8; John 20:24–29; 1 Corinthians 15:3–8)
- Ascended into Heaven and now sits at the right hand of God the Father. (Luke 22:69; Acts 1:1–9; Colossians 3:1)
- Promised to return to earth to judge all people, both living and dead. (Matthew 24:36–42; John 14:1–3; Acts 1:10–11, 10:39–42; 1 Peter 4:5)

  o Our family believes in *God the Holy Spirit*, who has been God's presence on earth from the beginning (Genesis 1:1–2) and who
  - Is an active and vital part of God. (John 16:5–15; Acts 1:7–8; Romans 8:26–27)
  - Lives and works in every baptized believer (Christian). (Acts 2:38; 1 Corinthians 3:16, 6:19; 2 Timothy 1:14)

- Our family believes in the *Bible*—God's message, His Holy Word (Scripture).
  o We believe God inspired the original writings of the 66 books of the Bible and those original writings were without error (inerrant). (Mark 12:36; John 14:26, 16:12–15; Acts 1:16; 1 Corinthians 2:12–13; 2 Timothy 3:14–16; 2 Peter 1:20–21)
  o Our family confirms the Bible as the final authority for all matters of faith and practice as it reveals God, God's vision, God's purposes, and God's Good News for all people (Isaiah 40:8; Matthew 5:18, 24:35; Romans 15:4; Hebrews 4:12)

- Our family believes the Bible teaches that all people
  o Are separated from God through sin. (Isaiah 59:2; Ephesians 4:18; Colossians 1:21)
  o Are without hope apart from God's saving grace through Jesus Christ. (Acts 4:12; Romans 3:23)

- Our family believes the Bible teaches that salvation (forgiveness of sin and reuniting with God) is *only* by grace (God's gift of salvation given without merit) through Jesus' sacrificial death and realized through relationship with Him. (Matthew 26:28; Romans 5:9; Ephesians 2:4–9; 1 Peter 1:18–19; 1 John 1:7)

- Our family believes the Bible teaches that one commits to this relationship with God and His grace by
    - Believing in and putting their faith in Christ. (John 11:25–26, 20:29, 20:31; Romans 5:1–2, 10:4, 10:9–10; Mark 16:16)
    - Repenting of sin (acknowledging and turning from sin). (Luke 24:45–47; Acts 3:19, 17:30; 2 Peter 3:9)
    - Confessing that Jesus Christ is Lord. (Matthew 10:32; Romans 10:9–13; Philippians 2:11; 1 John 4:15)
    - Being immersed (through baptism) into Christ. (Acts 2:38; Romans 6:1–7; Galatians 3:27; Colossians 2:12; 1 Peter 3:21)
- Our family believes that the Bible teaches that our committed relationship to God prompts a response from every believer (disciple). This response to our relationship with God inspires us to
    - Worship God. (2 Kings 17:28–39; Psalms 29:2, 95:6, 99:5, 99:9, 100:2; Matthew 4:10; John 4:20–24; Romans 12:1; Hebrews 12:28; Revelation 7:11, 14:7, 22:8–9)
    - Love each other in perfect unity. (John 13:34–35, 15:12, 17:20–23; 1 Corinthians 1:10; Colossians 3:12–14)
    - Grow spiritually. (Ephesians 4:11–16; Philippians 1:6, 3:12–15; Colossians 1:9–10; 2 Timothy 3:16–17; Hebrews 5:12–14, 6:1–2; 1 Peter 2:1–3; 2 Peter 3:17–18)
    - Share the good news (Gospel) of Jesus Christ to all people. (Matthew 28:18–20; Mark 16:15–16; Acts 4:18–20, 5:27–32, 5:40–42)
    - Serve others. (Acts 2:45; 2 Corinthians 9:6–15; 1 Peter 4:8–11)
- Our family believes the church (fellowship) of Jesus Christ (*God's family*) was
    - Founded by Christ. (Matthew 16:13–18)
    - Established after Christ's resurrection. (Acts 2:14–47)
    - Consists of *all* believers (Christians) everywhere. (Galatians 3:26–28)
- Our family believes the Bible teaches that the elders (shepherds) are the spiritual leaders and guides of the local church (God's family). (Acts 20:28; Philippians 1:1; 1 Timothy 3:1–7; Titus 1:5–9; 1 Peter 5:1–4)

Appendix F

FXCC Vision, Mission, Values

Our Vision—
To be God's Heart to this community.

We will be God's heart to this community. Connected to God, we will live beyond our abilities, fears, and imaginations. With God's power flowing through us, we commit to

- Deepen biblical understanding that produces greater spiritual maturity
  - By studying, teaching, and mentoring others. Spiritual maturity, passion, and commitment are marked by an ever-increasing desire to follow Christ wherever He leads and developed through the identification and use of gifts provided by the Holy Spirit to serve others. (Romans 12:3–7; 1 Corinthians 3:1–4; Ephesians 4:11–16; Hebrews 5:12; 1 Peter 2:1–3)
- Honor God as the center of our worship and invite others into His presence
  - By focusing on God, respecting our diversity as a gift from God, enriching our members, and welcoming our community. (Matthew 5:21–26; 1 Corinthians 12:1–31, 14:1–5, 14:23, 8:1–13)
- Make the most of our unique location for local and far-reaching spiritual impact

- - By capitalizing upon the transience in and around our nation's capital. We seek to spread the Good News of God to those who do not know it and to spiritually equip our members who move to other parts of the country or world. (1 Corinthians 9:19–27; Colossians 1:28–29)
- Provide a home for people seeking unconditional love, peace, belonging, and rest
  - By confessing we have been "born again" by the Holy Spirit into God's redefined family. We welcome believers as brothers and sisters in Christ into a home for anyone seeking to know and do God's will. (Matthew 12:48–50; Luke 4:18; John 13:35, 17:3; Galatians 6:1-4; Ephesians 3:1–6; 4:15)
- Reach out to diverse communities with the Good News of Jesus Christ
  - By seeking ways to lead as many people as possible to eternal life in Christ. We seek to daily touch the spiritual lives of others through care and support. (Psalm 9:9, 10:17–18; Luke 4:18–19; Romans 12:1–2; 1 Corinthians 9:19–27; Colossians 4:5; Hebrews 3:13; James 1:27;)

Our Mission

To boldly show Jesus, to love God, and to love others because God first loved us.

Our Values

The following values express our most passionate and unyielding priorities.

Connecting with God

by honoring Jesus Christ as the head of His church, yielding to the Bible as the Inspired Word of God, and faithfully worshipping God.

Connecting with Christians

by welcoming each other into a home for people seeking unconditional love, peace, belonging, and rest.

Connecting with Others

by sharing Christ's truth as a welcome into authentic Christian community.

FXCC exists to boldly obey the Great Commission and the Greatest Command by the power of the Greatest Truth.

- **The GREATEST Truth:** God Loves Us (John 3:16)
- **The GREATEST Command:** Love God and love others (Matthew 22:37–39)
- **The GREAT Commission:** Share the Good News (Matthew 28:19–20)